HINTERLAND

Hinterland offers an ans...
question 'what is creative...
by showcasing the best ne...
the fields of memoir, essay...... and
food writing, reportage, psychoscape,
biography, flash non-fiction and more.

Our pages bring together work by
established, award-winning authors
alongside new writers, many of whom
we are thrilled to publish for the first time
and whose work, we promise, will merit
your full attention.

Often, the pieces you'll find in Hinterland
will straddle the boundaries between
strands and be difficult to classify:
we see this as a strength. Hinterland
intends to challenge, move, entertain
and, above all, be a fantastic read.

WELCOME TO ISSUE 2

Advocates for Hinterland:
Trevor Goul-Wheeker, Nathan Hamilton, Rachel Hore,
Kathryn Hughes, Helen Smith, Rebecca Stott, Ian Thomson

Editorial Team
Editors-In-Chief   Freya Dean & Andrew Kenrick
Art Direction & Design   Tom Hutchings
Business Support   Ben Watkins
Readers   Susan K Burton, Aaron Deary, Margaret Hedderman,
Yin F Lim, Aaron O'Farrell, Stephen Massil

Submissions
Hinterland is committed to paying writers and artists for all work we publish.
Please send us your work via Submittable:
hinterlandnonfiction.submittable.com
We accept submissions year-round and endeavour to reply within 3 months.
We regret we are unable to provide feedback.
There is a small fee of £3 per submission.

Subscriptions
An annual subscription to Hinterland
(four issues, print and digital) costs £34 U.K.,
£44 Europe, £54 Rest-of-world.
Digital subscription only, £20.
Please visit our website for full details.

Distribution
Hinterland is distributed worldwide by NBN International.
For all trade orders contact +44 (0) 1752 202301
orders@nbninternational.com

Advertising
Please see our website for current rates, or to discuss sponsorship please
contact Andrew Kenrick at hinterlandnonfiction@gmail.com

Acknowledgments
The Editors gratefully acknowledge financial contributions from the UEA
Enterprise Santander fund and support from the UEA Publishing Project.

Find Hinterland online at
www.hinterlandnonfiction.com
or contact us: hinterlandnonfiction@gmail.com

ISBN: 978-1-911343-86-8
ISSN (Print): 2632-136X
ISSN (Online): 2632-1378

Copyright is reserved to the authors and artists, their heirs and executors.
All other text is copyright Hinterland Press Ltd.
Illustration on p16 by Rayne Van Dunem, used under Creative Commons Share Alike license
https://commons.wikimedia.org/wiki/File:Bercowcoatofarms.svg https://creativecommons.org/licenses/by-sa/3.0/

HINTERLAND

THE BEST NEW CREATIVE NON-FICTION

Issue 2
SUMMER
2019

Issue 2 / Summer 2019

Editorial

At time of writing our print run for Issue 1 is a handful of copies away from selling out and the number of submissions we've received has passed the 350 mark – not bad for a magazine that is still only a few months' old. The demand for a publication dedicated solely to non-fiction is clear; but what we've been even more thrilled by is the often daring nature of the work that we have received – whether that be in terms of theme, form or an alchemical melding of genres.

So, welcome to this second issue of Hinterland, which sees our writers continue to chart thrilling new ground in the realm of non-fiction. Let Richard Beard take you on a journey along The Archangel's Way, follow Antoinette Moses as she explores the possibilities of scriptwriting to describe real, historical events. Other work featured in this issue is equally far-flung in both time and place and lives up to our promise to bring you the best new non-fiction from around the globe. Nicholas Ward takes us back to one night in Chicago in a sharp, wistful tale of early manhood. Yin Lim revisits her native Malaysia and its cuisine, through the eyes of a tourist.

Freya Dean is of Dutch-British descent. She was an Elizabeth Kostova Foundation Finalist in 2017 and the recipient of the 2017/2018 Lorna Sage Award. Her work has appeared in *Visual Verse*, *The Writes of Woman* and *UEA's NonFiction Anthology*.

Sureshkumar P. Sekar pens a love-letter to the music of A.R. Rahman, Roger Cranse revisits a troubling boyhood encounter and Kate Romain takes us on an awkward second date. Family history is central to both Kinga Cybulska's *On Krakowskie Przedmieście* and Katie Simpson's *This Is Not A Ghost Story But A Haunting*, and in each case these writers describe that past in richly layered, unexpected ways. In our regular *Brief Lives* feature, Stephen Massil puts John Bercow under the lens in a beautifully distilled piece of biography. Equally topical, our photo essay this month comes from Martin Eberlen on the subject of climate change, while our interview with Bart van Es, author of *The Cut Out Girl*, turns around the legacy of post-war Europe, reinventing the biographical form, and the work of W.G. Sebald.

All this alongside a selection of flash non-fiction that does just what flash pieces should: dazzle, unsettle, delight – and leave you wanting more. Enjoy!

Freya Dean & Andrew Kenrick
Editors-in-Chief

Andrew Kenrick has worked as an archaeologist and an archivist, a writer and an editor. He is currently studying for a PhD at the University of East Anglia, where he is researching new ways to write biographies of ancient figures.

Contributors

Richard Beard
(*The Archangel's Way*) has written six novels and four books of narrative non-fiction. His memoir *The Day That Went Missing* won the 2018 PEN Ackerley Award for literary autobiography and was a finalist for the National Book Critics Circle Award.

Roger Conant Cranse
(*National Newark and Essex*) was born and raised in New Jersey. He graduated from Rutgers University in 1963 and served in the US Peace Corps in Nepal and Vietnam. His memoir, *The Hearts and Minds Guys*, about his experiences during the Vietnam war appeared in *Raritan* and was named a Notable Essay in The Best American Essays of 2013. Roger has spent most of his career teaching at the Community College of Vermont, where he also lives.

Kinga Elwira Cybulska
(*On Krakowskie Przedmieście*) was born in Eastern Europe. She has lived in Kraków, Galway and London, and currently works as a bookseller. She earned her MA in Polish Literature and Language, studied Journalism at Jagiellonian University; and Creative Writing at Cambridge University and UEA. She has contributed to the anthology of immigrant poetry *Landing Places* and *Galway: City of Strangers*. Her non-fiction has been published in *Machina*, *Zadra* and *Ale Historia*.

Spencer Darr

(*The Night's Content Moderation Watch*) is a non-fiction writer currently focusing on the relationships between people, love and technology. His work has appeared in *Atlas Obscura* and *The Nervous Breakdown*. A first generation college grad from Pecan Hill, Texas, USA, he is pursuing an MFA in Creative Writing with an emphasis in Literary Nonfiction at University of Nevada, Las Vegas.

Bart van Es

(*In Conversation With*) was born in the Netherlands and grew up in Norway, Dubai, Indonesia and the U.K. He studied English Literature at Cambridge and is now Professor of English at Oxford. His academic books include *Shakespeare in Company* and *Shakespeare's Comedies*. In 2014 van Es began to look into his family's wartime history, knowing that a Jewish girl, Lien, had lived in hiding with his grandparents during the occupation. He met Lien, now aged 82, and began the first of a series of interviews that formed the basis for *The Cut Out Girl*; which won the Costa Book of the Year 2018 and the Slightly Foxed First Biography Prize. Translations are out or forthcoming in fourteen languages.

Martin Eberlen (*There Are No Polar Bears Where I Live*) is a London-based documentary photographer, visual artist and writer. Martin graduated in 2018 with a distinction from the MA Photojournalism and Documentary Photography course at London College of Communication and the same year was selected, with just thirty other artists from around the globe, to be part of Parallel Photo Platform. As part of a year-long cycle, these artists create a new body of work to be exhibited in various European cities.

Caroline Gardam (*The Common Mango*) is a writer and editor based in south-east Queensland, Australia. Her work has been published in magazines and newspapers across Australia, including *Meanjin*. She holds a Graduate Diploma in Arts (Writing, Editing, and Publishing) from the University of Queensland.

Richard Horne (*You Are Here*) is a graphic designer, illustrator, author, screen and gocco printer. His books include the best selling *101 Things To Do Before You Die* series and the *Modern Day Spotter's Guide* amongst others. He also illustrated the best selling *The Dangerous Book for Boys*, winner of the 2007 book of the year at the British Book Awards. His clients include The National Trust, *Guardian & Guardian Guide*, UEA, Comic Relief, Harper Collins, Penguin Random House, Universal Music, Warner Music and the V&A Museum.

Tom Hutchings is our in-house graphic designer and photographer, based in the south of London. A brand new father, Tom is currently wishing for a few more hours in the day to get some extra sleep. Have a look at his varied output at www.thorngraphicdesign.com.

Nicole Im
(*Twelve and Holding*) was born and raised in California. Her work has appeared in *Freeman's Journal*, *Literary Hub* and *The Huffington Post*. She holds an MFA in Creative Non-fiction from The New School and is currently working on a memoir. Visit her at www.nicoleim.com.

Yin F. Lim
(*Tourist in My Homeland*) is a Malaysian-born writer and editor who is now based in the UK. Interested in food, family stories and the East Asian diaspora, her work has been published in several anthologies including *Who Are We Now? A Collection of True Stories about Brexit*. Find her at yinflim.com and on Twitter @YinFLim.

Dru Marland
(*The Archangel's Way*) is a poet, illustrator and mechanic. She lives among the voles on the Kennet and Avon Canal.

Stephen Massil
(*Mr Speaker Bercow, Man of the People*) held a senior position at the University of London Library, which he combined with postings at the Huguenot Library, Sir John Soane's Museum, the National Trust and the Garrick Club. He is a Vice-President of the Jewish Historical Society of England, a Fellow of the Society of Antiquaries and of the Library Association; and a contributor to the *Oxford Dictionary of National Biography*. In 2016 he gained an MA in Biography and Creative Non-Fiction from UEA, where his principal subject was *Lost Cousins*, chronicling a series of historical figures and their connections, with an autobiographical undertow.

Antoinette Moses
(*Whose Play Is It Anyway?*) is
an author who has published
over twenty books of award-
winning language-learner
literature. She is also a
playwright with a PhD in
documentary theatre and has
recently retired from teaching
creative writing at UEA and
producing the Festival of
Literature for Young people
(FLY), which she co-founded
in 2013. She previously
worked for the Norfolk and
Norwich Festival, re-founded
and ran the Cambridge
Animation Festival and
helped set up the Hiroshima
Animation Festival. In 2016
Antoinette published the first
extract of her memoirs in
Words and Women 3.

Allison Pugh
(*I Need to Know How to Hard
Boil an Egg*) is a writer from
North Central West Virginia
who resides in Chesapeake.
She earned her MFA from
West Virginia Wesleyan
College in 2015 and is a
fiction editor at *Heartwood*,
a literary magazine in
association with WVWC.
This is her first published piece.

Kate Romain
(*Parasites and Autoclaves*) is an
Anglo-American writer of
both fiction and non-fiction.
She recently completed
an MA in Biography and
Creative Non-fiction at
the University of East
Anglia before somewhat
spontaneously relocating to
Ann Arbor, Michigan, where
she currently resides.

Sureshkumar P. Sekar
(*Rahmania*) is a writer from
Salem, India. He studied
mechanical engineering and
worked as a software engineer
for thirteen years before
gaining his MA in Creative
Writing from the University
of East Anglia in 2018. He
is currently working on a
hybrid musicological memoir,
Leitmotif, and a monograph
on Indian film scores, *The
Music of Lagaan*. He will
shortly begin doctoral study
on film music at the Royal
College of Music, London.

Katie Simpson
(*This Is Not A Ghost Story
But A Haunting*) is a writer
and photographer in San
Francisco. Her work has
been featured in *Eastern
Iowa Review*, *Boston Accents*,
and *Entropy Magazine* among
others. You can find her on
Twitter @honest_creative.

Nicholas Ward's
(*Nacional 27*) writing has
appeared with *The Billfold*,
Bird's Thumb, *Catapult*,
Midwestern Gothic, *Vol. 1 Brooklyn*,
HowlRound, and others. He
is a company member with
2nd Story, a Chicago-based
storytelling collective, and
the Booking Manager at
Young Chicago Authors.

HINTERLAND

At Hinterland we are committed to
publishing the best in creative non-fiction
from around the globe.

We are always thrilled to feature work
from established, well-known authors but
have a particular interest in discovering
new voices and in pieces that sit outside
the usual categories: we ask only that
it be a work of non-fiction.

We operate an open, year-round
submissions policy and aim to read
all work submitted within three months.

We pay for all the work that we publish
and receive frequent interest from agents
and publishers regarding our contributors.

Please send us your best work and we
will endeavour to find a place for it.

Guidelines for submissions

- Submissions should be made via Submittable only. Please follow the link below:

- A small fee of £3 per submission applies to non-subscribers. Subscribers enjoy the benefit of submitting their work for free.

- All work should be new, previously unpublished material. If your work is subsequently accepted elsewhere, please kindly let us know.

- Pieces should not run to more than 5000 words. We accept anything from 500 words (very short pieces will be considered for our flash non-fiction slot). We also accept extracts from longer works, or works in progress.

- We warmly embrace writing on any topic, or from any genre, we ask only that it falls somewhere in the realm of non-fiction writing.

- Your work will be considered for all upcoming issues; it might help you to know that we operate a 3-4 month editorial lead time.

- We regret that, due to the number of submissions received, we cannot provide feedback.

hinterland.submittable.com/submit

Brief Lives

John Bercow's coat of arms, designed by Hubert Chesshyre
[late Clarenceux King of Arms]

Mr Speaker Bercow, Man of the People

by Stephen Massil

Two women got onto my bus this morning with a
child in a pushchair. The mother called the boy
'Jonah' who, before long had noticed a stationary
lorry with scaffolders' ladders strapped up. He made
efforts to gain a better view and, as she explained
to her friend and the woman to her right, ladders
are the boy's fetish at the moment. Ladders are
among my own current preoccupations too, having
a copy of the Speaker's armorial in my writing-
case, wondering at its multiple resonances. I passed
it to the mother and boy, who received it with
enthusiasm. The boy promptly counted the steps.
The affinities for a Jonah of a Jacob's ladder are
not hard to find. Mr Speaker Bercow would surely
have favoured the Herald's secondary allusion when

giving focus to such a ladder in a scutcheon by which to record taking the steady steps of a career over time. Not for such a Speaker the greasy-pole of political ambition but the conversation during the ascent and progress by degrees.

We are wished one-hundred-and-twenty years for valour. Long life is brief in the scale of things; each step of the ladder a life in itself. My godfather Lewis Austin was a one-term Member for Stretford under the Attlee government (the Earl Winterton being Father of the House, Member for Horsham – baby of the House on his first election in 1904 – and the Speaker Douglas Clifton Brown, Member for Hexham). He came to supper in the early summer of 1948 to give me, ahead of my autumn birthday, a cricket bat. As a furniture-maker he had an eye for timber and the appreciation of the sleek willow for the play over several summers at school. This gift afforded me privileges in the school playground, distributing favours of the bat to whichever team was at the stumps. My early school reports defer to my reliability regarding the rules of all the games of the playground.

John Bercow was a tennis champion and had Bobby Wilson as his coach; the same Wilson whose exploits (when I was at school in Finchley) gave rise to half-day holidays during Wimbledon over several years when he fought successive quarter-finals, following a second-round defeat by Jaroslav Drobný in 1952. This was a decade before Bercow was born and a further decade before he was stricken with bronchial asthma over the last winter of his junior status and gave up competition, being short of training.

When he brought his young family to Parliament during the votes for the speakership in 2009, he was aware that his elderly mother was keenly interested in the proceedings going forward under the chairmanship of Alan Williams (Member for Swansea West). At the commencement of each subsequent Parliament, the Fathers of the House were respectively Sir Geoffrey Tapsell (Louth & Horncastle), Sir Gerald Kaufman (Gorton), and Kenneth Clarke (Rushcliffe). There was no election as such on these occasions, rather an invitation to Mr Bercow to recommend himself afresh for appointment as Speaker by acclaim as a 'tested' candidate *par excellence*, glad to learn and to teach in the role. His speeches at this point were gracious and witty, replete with the *douceurs* of Parliamentary deference, courtesies and dignity, ready with self-deprecation but also with resolve; in his fourth term he now carries gravitas and confidence to a pitch. He is unabashed, unembarrassed; he conveys reassurance and demonstrates his mastery of the chamber for the management of the House and its estate and of the Orders and service of the day.

John Bercow gave us a brief resumé of his background when he came to speak to Charles Clarke on the University of East Anglia campus in 2015. He referred to his early Tory zeal under the influence of Enoch Powell and Margaret Thatcher when still a schoolboy – something he has since disclaimed, along with other 'bone-headed views' held in his minority. It seemed significant that his Berkowitz grandparents had been immigrants to London, but that his father

Charles Bercow would not talk about those days of his boyhood and other such things and that they had died before his parents' marriage (in 1956). His mother, Brenda Bailey (born in 1928), from Huddersfield, was the daughter of an unmarried mother; and you can learn online that she was a convert to Judaism. You can discover also that the Berkowitz family came from Romania – but that's not enough in the context of tracing a man's life, background and focus of character. Was that by rail from Transylvania across the Austro-Hungarian empire? Were they from Iaşi or Vaslui west of the River Prut? Or from Moldavia, neighbourly to Bessarabia (from where my own maternal grandmother hailed), or from Bucharest itself – all Jewish centres with a horizon towards Odessa in the way of cultural transmigration, and embarkation over the Black Sea?

Mr Speaker Bercow rises to multiple roles in the course of his duties and in their performance. He is as aware of the traditions of the Savoy Opera and the pantomime of Gilbert's parliamentary tropes from which the cartoonists derive their imagery, as of the thrill of Shakespearean debate. Parliament, the Commons, is a school playground. The Speaker has the *manège* of the unruly 'voices' – the 'mob' of *Julius Caesar* – and the measure of the *Honourable* Members who have to be brought to heel (outdoing *Pius* Aeneas, and *Honest* Iago with the edge of the inherent sarcasm implied). With his deputies and clerks he has mastery of all the rules and the decorum – the 'Order' – of the House and its service. He knows the names of all the members, and their constituencies, on all sides of the House. As a 'listener' to debate (and close reader of *Hansard*) he has the measure of their usual utterances; he can detect their attempts to steal a march on procedure; he can explain himself at all points; he can remind them of what they said 'last time' and where they misquote themselves. From his 'conversation' with Charles Clarke it is evident that he might mimic even their voices (well, not to their faces in the Chamber – that would not be honourable), protean in exposition as in thought. Above all he is insistent on due process and the rights of the speaker of the moment to be heard, whether at the despatch box or from the benches, being threatened by the unruly – not for nothing was Bercow's father a taxi-driver who will have been heard on *every* occasion.

John Bercow has been Member for Buckingham since 1997 and Speaker (for what is now a record number of terms) since June 2009. He has constituents who deplore his prolonged absence, but these voices fail to appreciate the honour of being represented in Parliament by such a man in that office; he enfranchises them by his position, his eloquence, his opinions and his dedication to the routines of the House. When introduced for the fourth time after the General Election of 2017, his sponsor Cheryl Gillan (Chesham and Amersham) repeated several of the anecdotes used on such an occasion – the one that drew the loudest response from the Floor came when she referred to the seven incumbents of the deep Parliamentary past who had been beheaded.

'More,' they bayed with glee.

Another likely resonance of the Herald's image of the ladder conveys an allusion to Bercow's diminutive stature, not withheld in the hubbub of Parliament and the media. Mr Bercow himself is not averse to urging his height, letting the processional swagger carry the point for him, wearing robes magnifying their gloss of Office. Those who recognise his mastery of his role view him as a giant in office. It is said that Isaac Newton's claim to have attained his view of the universe by standing on the shoulders of giants is fraught with a spasm of his rivalry in the early years of the Royal Society with Mr Hooke, of the *Micrographia* (1665), regarded as a man of small physical stature, great in mind and achievement in science.

At this point in his career, confirmed again in the Speaker's chair, John Bercow is intent on modernising the procedures of the House, to entertain the primacy of back-benchers, and of Parliament, and to befit the place of the first man of the people which the seat affords. Mr Bercow impresses the viewer and confronts the ranged members gazing and wondering at his eloquence and articulation in argument, deploying the 'words of learned length' like the Parson in Oliver Goldsmith's *The Deserted Village*, with 'thund'ring sound.' **H**

The Common Mango

Caroline Gardam

There's this guy who lives on my street. Called
Dutch. Rides a motorbike. Looks like the type of
cat who's already gone through a few of his nine
lives. Lives in the front half of a rented place at the
bottom of the hill.

Dutch, of course, is not his actual name.
I don't know what name he was given at birth.
I asked him once; he laughed at me. I don't know
how long he's lived on this street: longer than us.
He's good for a chat.

Out the front of Dutch's place was a magnificent
gnarly old tree, one of those old-school, no-nonsense
common mangoes. The kind whose fruit is good
for Asian salads and daiquiris but too stringy to
eat straight up: no competition for those designer
mango brands trucked down from Far North
Queensland. This tree, a densely canopied beauty
whose blossoms cranked the birds: its leaves threw
the coolest shade. Dutch, you could tell, was proud
of 'his' tree. (Quaintly contra-character, the way he
called it 'my tree'. Un-tough.)

It's how I met him, originally – I think it's how
half the neighbourhood met him – when one
summer I picked my way through the used bike
parts decorating his front path to ask if I could
please pick some of the green fruit to make a salad?
It became a summer ritual, picking Dutch's green

mangoes. Heaps of us did it. I made salads (Dutch's mangoes were always in a salad on our Christmas table), others made pickles. Standing on the footpath outside; I once watched a cheeky Vietnamese-Australian woman drive up, park beneath the tree and unload its branches from the bonnet of her car. Last year, Dutch's neighbour stood on his own car bonnet to pick late-season fruit for me.

The tree was Dutch's conduit to the community. A sweet crack in tough-guy exterior.

And mangoes for all. This year promised to be the best yet: just last month, the tree was so fecund with blossom I 'grammed it. We were excited.

Then this week, walking down the street, I become muddled in my bearings. One of those shaky virtual-reality-like moments slowed my feet, until I stop outside a house I couldn't quite recognize. The massive old mango has vanished.

Later, I see Dutch, ask what happened. He looks sad. He says he has no idea. Woke one morning and 'a couple of tree guys' were on his front lawn. Someone had complained about the mango to his landlord. He didn't know what sort of complaint. Blossom dropping? Says if they'd just spoken to him, he would have taken some branches off the front if they were in anyone's way (they weren't) – it's what he did each year, just hadn't got around to it yet. Says he wishes his landlord had spoken to him about it. Says he's not sure what to plant in its place. Says he thought it might get a bit hot, his house, this summer.

We discuss the tree's unprecedented blossom.
Shake our heads. I say I have a frangipani in a pot,
if he wants it.

The November sun, glaring across his bare front
yard, hurts my eyes. ◫

The Night's Content Moderation Watch Oath

Spencer Darr

Night gathers somewhere online, and now my watch begins.[1] It shall not end until the death of my contract.[2] I shall take no spouse,[3] hold no mortgage, and have no children see what I have seen.[4] I shall wear no crowns and win no job security.[5] My innocence shall live and die at my two-screened post.[6] I am the watcher in the server walls.[7] I am the flag that takes down illegal content,[8] the light that moderates the dark web,[9] the alarm that wakes the authorities,[10] the shield that guards the free speech of users.[11] I pledge my working life and honor to The Night's Content Moderation Watch, for this night and all the nights to come.[12] **H**

1 Glaser, April. 'Want a Terrible Job? Facebook and Google May Be Hiring.' *Slate Magazine*, 18th January 2018, slate.com/technology/2018/01/facebook-and-google-are-building-an-army-of-content-moderators-for-2018.html

2 Crosbie, Jack. 'Facebook's 3,000 New Moderators Won't Get Full-Time Jobs.' *Inverse*, 6th May 2017, www.inverse.com/article/31130-facebook-live-murder-moderators-part-time-contractors

3 Blair, Olivia. 'Millennials Are Shunning Marriage and Children for Education and a Career, Says Report.' *The Independent*, 21st April 2017, www.independent.co.uk/life-style/millenials-marriage-children-higher-education-career-jobs-report-united-states-census-bureau-a7695881.html

4 Singh, Anita. 'Facebook Moderators "Develop PTSD Because They Are Exposed to the Worst Content on the Internet."' *The Telegraph*, 31st May 2017, www.telegraph.co.uk/news/2017/05/31/facebookmoderators-develop-ptsd-exposed-worst-content-internet

5 Solon, Olivia. 'Underpaid and Overburdened: the Life of a Facebook Moderator.' *The Guardian*, 25th May 2017, www.theguardian.com/news/2017/may/25/facebook-moderator-underpaid-overburdened-extreme-content

6 Chen, Adrian. 'The Laborers Who Keep Dick Pics and Beheadings Out of Your Facebook Feed.' *Wired*, 23rd October 2014, www.wired.com/2014/10/content-moderation

7 Lardinois, Frederic. 'A Look inside Facebook's Data Center.' *TechCrunch*, 13th July 2016, techcrunch.com/gallery/a-look-inside-facebooks-data-center

8 'Sexual Violence and Exploitation: How We Fight Sexual Violence and Exploitation on Facebook.' *Community Standards, Facebook*, March 2018, https://www.facebook.com/communitystandards

9 Valentine, Ben. 'The Stories of Content Moderators, Hosted on the Darknet.' *Hyperallergic*, 11th February 2016, hyperallergic.com/271703/the-stories-of-content-moderators-hosted-on-the-darknet

10 'Criminal Activity: How We Handle Reports of Criminal Activity on Facebook.' *Community Standards, Facebook*, March 2018, https://www.facebook.com/communitystandards

11 Solon, Olivia. 'To Censor or Sanction Extreme Content? Either Way, Facebook Can't Win.' *The Guardian*, 23rd May 2017, www.theguardian.com/news/2017/may/22/facebook-moderator-guidelines-extreme-content-analysis

12 The piece was inspired by preparation for my new job working the graveyard shift as a Content Moderator on contract with Facebook in Austin, TX. This pastiche takes from both versions of 'The Night's Watch Oath' from Episode 7, Season 1 of the HBO television series *Game of Thrones*, which is an adaptation of the original oath from the fantasy novel *A Game of Thrones* by George R.R. Martin. Both versions of the oath can be found here: http://iceandfire.wikia.com/wiki/Night%27s_Watch

Afternoon Light

Scott Russell Morris

A quiet afternoon at home, the morning's chores done and Kirsten's at work. I open all the windows in the living room to let in the low, early winter light, warm on our gray walls and cream carpets. Outside, beige leaves blow across the driveway and the Texas-brown lawn, but it all feels gold today and our white couch soaks up the heat – it spills out to the red and aqua rug. It's just me and Cal, our one-year-old, who normally so wiggly, is extra cuddly, sick with a fever. He announces the end of his nap with a quiet whimper – usually a throaty, lung-deep cry – and I pick him up, cradling him as I prepare his bottle.

On the couch he curls in close, his fever not as high as it was this morning, but still his body warms up mine, and I feel sweat in the crook of my arm, inside my elbows, as his pink hands grasp the bottle and he suckles down the formula. I put my hand up his shirt and rub his warm belly, feeling the heat rising from it, savoring its smoothness, thinking how nice it is to have a quiet child on a warm winter afternoon.

We sit like this for several moments, everything as calm as it could ever be, thinking, perhaps, of the Ray LaMontange lyrics ... I could hold you forever.

He finishes the bottle and closes his eyes. I close mine too, glad for the continued quiet, a chance to rest from a long night and a busy morning. He feels warmer now. Cal whimpers a little and I settle us deeper into the couch and the afternoon light, laying out in full, his body still cradled in my arm, his weight resting against my chest, his head on my shoulder.

A gurgle of a cough and I open my eyes to see his body tense, his lips blue, his breathing faint and I jump up, clutching him, turning him over, thinking he's choking, but he's not choking and his whole face is flushed violet now and his eyes roll up, his body subtly shaking and I think, I've killed him, I've killed him and scramble for my phone to call an ambulance, though I don't know where it is; I stutter through the house, room to room to room, while my baby shakes breathlessly in my arms, and though the doctors will later tell us that febrile seizures are common in children this young and that the correct treatment is to lay them on their side and wait, no one has prepared me for this moment, where I am clutching him to me in the perse dim of the hallway and whispering half-prayers, purple prayers that hardly leave my mouth, aborted prayers and yet still the closest to the true nature of prayer I've ever come, nothing vain at all in my repetition:

Oh God. Oh God. Oh God. ◧

I Need To Know How To Hard Boil An Egg

Allison Pugh

How many minutes in the water, how much vinegar?
Do I peel them while warm, or is it easier if they've
cooled? It's dill relish for deviled eggs. Or is it sweet? Pick
up the phone. Hear the dial tone on the cordless before
I remember there's no one to answer it. Hang up. Find
a Google answer. The eggs are overcooked anyhow.

The midday news ignores my desire to see what the
weather will be tomorrow and talks instead of the anniversary
of Pearl Harbor. December 7th is my grandmother's
birthday, but there's no address to send a card to.

The baby's sleeping so I try to write. About moving
to Virginia, how my leaving mirrors my grandmother's
same exodus; but I don't remember when she moved
to Hampton. She only told me that one time. Right
before we went to Buckroe Beach. Never gave the
year, just the why, and I am trying to remember –

There it is again. The refrigerator and its
humming. Always in the quiet spaces. The rattle
that comes before and after the fridge does whatever
it is that reminds me of oxygen machines.

My daughter doesn't need something to breathe
for her anymore, but she does need more milk – and
the dog needs to go out and dinner needs fixing and
the world goes on no matter how many times your
grandmother has died again today. **H**

Twelve and Holding

Nicole Im

'There's nothing to be afraid of,' Mom says as we
pull out of our driveway. 'They're just going to take
some pictures of your brain. Like an X-ray.'

I have a 10 am appointment for an MRI at our
local radiology clinic. I am 12. For a moment, our
car faces Lindsey's house, and I hold my breath
until we turn once again and begin driving in the
opposite direction. When I think of Lindsey, I see
her face pressed close into mine. Her freckles are
magnified and her eyes bore holes into my face. I
remember the sex games she used to make me play
with her in her closet.

It's our secret, she'd tell me. *Stop crying. You can't go
home until you stop crying.*

For the last couple of months, I've been telling
Mom that I feel like I'm in a dream and can't wake
up. I told her I felt disconnected from everything, as
if everyone were standing far away. I'd already been
to the pediatrician, otolaryngologist, audiologist,
and even a local homeopath. It will never occur to
either of my parents to try a therapist. My dad is
the kind of man who rolls his eyes at antidepressant
commercials.

'Depression is for suckers,' I blurt out one day as
an ad for a you-can-stop-feeling-sad-if-you-take-this
medication comes on the screen – a woman unable
to get out of bed, the same woman staring forlornly

out a window, her only comfort a cup of tea. I am terrified that the woman I see is the woman I will become; and I hope that by mocking what scares me, I can shame it away. Dad laughs and I bask in his approval.

'Do you feel dizzy?' Mom asks.

I scrunch my face and shake my head in time to the tick of our car's left-turn signal. 'Sort of, maybe.' I wish there is some other way I could describe how I feel, but there isn't. I feel like I am spinning farther and farther from everything and everyone I know. I feel like there is someone else inside my body and that my brain is floating above me; as if the real me is asleep somewhere, waiting to be woken up, and when I finally do, I'll realize that everything I've been living up until now isn't real. I'll realize that we don't live next door to Lindsey – that we never have – that we were never even friends and I've never been inside her house, inside her closet. I like pretending that I am far away from Lindsey, but sometimes Mom seems far away too, and that scares me.

I want the doctors to tell me what's wrong, but I'm afraid they're going to tell me that my brain isn't normal. They'll look into my head and tell me what I already know: *there is something wrong with you.*

Mom parks the car under a sign that reads 'Modesto Radiology Imaging.' Inside the office, she fills out the patient form and we both sign at the bottom. A nurse sticks me with an IV and suddenly I am lying inside a long tube with a plastic cage around my face.

'Don't be scared, honey,' the technician tells me. 'Just relax.'

I want to rip the cage off my face, yank the needle out of my arm and run, but I force myself to lie still. The technician tells me he is using the IV to send dye into my bloodstream so that the doctors can read my brain scans. I feel a chill spread up my arm and wonder if the next time I get a paper cut, my blood will come out black.

One week later, Mom gets a call.

'The scans came back clear,' she tells me. 'How are you feeling now?'

'A little better, I guess.'

Mom looks relieved.

When Dad comes home from work, he hands me an article from one of his golf magazines. One side of the glossy page is jagged where it has been torn out.

'She has the same exact thing as you!' he says excitedly. 'And she's OK now!'

The article features a woman wearing a Nike visor and holding a golf club with a big smile on her face. The caption reads 'A virus left me with vertigo.' She talks about how she had a rare inner ear virus that threw off her balance. It was so bad that the woman couldn't walk in a straight line and she would vomit from feeling so nauseous. Eventually, though, her body healed and readjusted its center of alignment. 'My game has never been better!' she says at the end. Her story doesn't sound like mine at all. I try handing it back to Dad.

'Keep it for inspiration,' he says. 'I saved it for you.'

I fold the article into a tiny square and hide it at the back of my desk drawer. ⊞

The

Archangel's

Way

by Richard Beard
Illustrated by Dru Marland

Walking is easy. Most people do it on a regular basis, free of charge and with a simple aim in mind: to get from one place to another. Make the walk a pilgrimage, and everything changes. The walk now has a purpose and a spiritual destination. Enlightenment is within reach.

Any number of walker-writers have enjoyed the self-importance of a pilgrimage, but Rebecca Solnit can speak for us all. 'Pilgrimage –' she writes in *Wanderlust*, '– is almost universally embedded in human culture as a literal means of a spiritual journey.'

Unfortunately, my friend Dru Marland and I have only a couple of days spare for endeavours of existential significance. Santiago de Compostela will have to wait. As will the ritual Hindu pilgrimage recommended for the over-fifties, an age neither of us will see again. Instead, our act of pilgrimage is going to take place in Devon, on a newly dedicated trail called the Archangel's Way.

The provisional route covers about twenty-five kilometres of mixed terrain between two churches of St Michael, the first at Brent Tor and the second at Chagford, which according to the website visitchagford.com is 'the prettiest town on Dartmoor.' Other walks are available, especially in this part of the world, but none of them have been plotted by 'the clergy who work on the moor,' a group of rural vicars who sound magical and slightly sinister.

In reality, the Reverend Adrian Brook of the Dartmoor parish of Bridestowe is quick to welcome us into his modern vicarage. Dog-collared, short-sleeve-shirted, his office is unashamedly from the clutter-and-welcome wing of the Church of England; the room dominated by an immense commercial photocopier that is printing out, very slowly, the route to Chagford as pencilled onto an Ordnance Survey map. We're early adopters, walking the route before it officially opens, so it seems fair to ask for guidance. We need to be told why we're doing this and how it's good for

> **We need to be told why we're doing this and how it's good for us. because really I ought to be back at my desk finishing a book. I need a justification, possibly divine. for the act of going for a walk**

us, because really I ought to be back at my desk finishing a book. I need a justification, possibly divine, for the act of going for a walk.

Dru has other reservations. She lives on a boat and time away is always filled with jeopardy: her home may be gone when she gets back, or disrupted in some important way. In a vicar's office, I realize, as if by an infectious habit of thought, every reflection risks becoming a sermon. Which is good preparation for the imagined lessons ahead of us, I feel, although at this stage Adrian is being more literal than metaphorical. He explains that the Archangel's Way is a re-imagined section of what was once the Cornish Celtic Way, a hike from St Michael's Mount to the south as far as

Glastonbury to the north. Our Devon section follows the same leylines so 'will be interesting to our pagan friends,' but Anglicanism is a broad church so as pilgrims we can find whatever we want. Depends what we're looking for but, according to Adrian, the Archangel's Way serves a demand for spiritual as well as physical refreshment. The path encompasses holy wells and ancient monuments via the regular spiritual punctuation of Dartmoor village churches.

In a piece of shameless foreshadowing, Adrian tells us that Dartmoor has 'a history of spiritual encounter.' The moor allows walkers to move closer to Nature and to God, and speaks to a re-emerging desire for spiritual experience in the fresh air outside the walls of organised religion. See? In the vicarage the metaphors are pervasive, though the general idea is that we'll reconnect to outpaced ideas by slowing to an ancient pace. Not just a walk, but a pilgrimage. Or, in the acronym coined by one of Solnit's walking friends, we're about to set off on an AFGO: Another Fucking Growth Opportunity.

But how will we know we're not just walking? By keeping in mind the metaphorical journey at all times, and the opportunities for inner transformation. Or, as Solnit puts it, 'walking is work.' The original guiding light of the allegorical English pilgrimage is John Bunyan, author of *The Pilgrim's Progress*, a book that has not been out of print since publication in 1678. As a seventeenth-century Puritan, Bunyan is an unlikely bedfellow for Rebecca Solnit, but he also wrote the words to

the famous hymn where he fears not what men say. Instead, he'll labour night and day, to be a pilgrim. For Bunyan as for Solnit, pilgrim-walking is labour, because personal inquiry and self-improvement are Puritan imperatives that endure. We're not walking for fun, but to save our incomplete selves.

While we're at it, we can assess the spiritual health of Dartmoor's inhabitants. Adrian tells us that pilgrimage tests the Christian tradition of hospitality, and we're fine with allowing his parishioners to be hospitable to us in any way they choose. As we leave the vicarage I even have it in my head that some kind of bylaw, of which I don't know the details, obliges an English home-owner to give a stranger water and let them use a toilet.

'Unlikely to be law,' Dru says.

'Maybe it was a law when they had outside toilets.'

'I don't think it's a law.'

Our battered packs show we're not at home. We're obvious outsiders. Because Dru is used to the cold from the boat she's wearing several layers of skirted carpets. She also has a shoulder-high blackthorn staff with a polished pommel, as if in homage to the pagan underlay of the route. If pilgrimage is a process of preparing, journeying and arriving, we have skimped on the preparation – but inappropriate gear suits the pilgrim mindset. This isn't sport walking, searching for efficiencies, and Dru is very proud of the highly inefficient can of corned beef she has decided to pack in her rucksack. And because one thing leads to another, she also has an unsliced loaf, butter, cheese and a solar power battery charger with no cable.

We are, however, lucky with the weather, and in breezy sunshine we start off by looking inside the hill-top church at Brent Tor ('Welcome to our church. Please help yourself to a drink of water and a packet of biscuits.') Eating biscuits, looking at the stained-glass St Michael, we remind ourselves virtuously that a pilgrimage is not a route march or a competition: a study of the A4 map pages fresh from the vicarage printer suggests the first seven kilometres is best negotiated in the car.

Because Dru is used to the cold from the boat she's wearing several layers of skirted carpets. She also has a shoulder-high blackthorn staff with a polished pommel, as if in homage to the pagan underlay of the route

Which takes us to the small man-made labyrinth beside the church of St Thomas à Becket at Sourton. We make up for the cheating by walking the narrow circular lanes several times. Laid out in a straight line, the labyrinth would amount to about a twenty-metre stretch of grass, but the inner journey is much longer. Here come the metaphors again, and the difference between a maze and a labyrinth offers two competing versions of life. A maze is a branching puzzle with choices of path and direction, including multiple exits and dead ends. A labyrinth has a single, non-branching path, which leads to the centre then back out the same way, with one possible entry and exit.

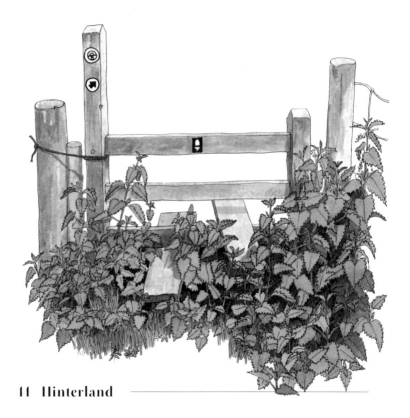

44 Hinterland

I don't know which is the more accurate description. It's only the start of the walk and I haven't had the opportunity to reflect. Also, as another adventure begins, we forget the deeper meanings and just have fun. From Sourton, the first part of the route follows a disused railway and, as the moor opens up, Dru goes through her mental encyclopedia of naturalist knowledge. She names every bird we hear and see, like a God proud of her creation: lark, willow warbler, a pair of wheatears back from Africa. Dru creates the birds for me by making me pay attention.

We're heading to the village of Belstone, which for me is another distraction from the natural world that Dru inhabits so easily. I'm both here and not here because as a child *The Belstone Fox* was among the first novels I read. In the story's major dramatic incident the fox outwits the hunt and leads the chasing hounds into the path of an express train. This must be the same railway line, made safe for hikers, but that book and film confused a generation of animal-loving children by making us side with the fox. Along with *The Belstone Fox*, *Tarka the Otter* was another Devonian environmental influence – foxes and otters were people too. I'd like to be more like Dru, appreciating animals and birds for the non-anthropomorphic miracle they are.

Once off the railway the slopes to the moor are bright with yellow gorse.

'Lucky us,' I say, but apparently not because Dru has a rhyme for it.

'When gorse is out of bloom, kissing's out of fashion.'

Which certainly doesn't apply to this invigorating April day in which the sunshine invites springtime thoughts of starting afresh. The season is entering its easy annual metaphor stage, but on the long uphill drag we talk about aeroplanes and children and depression, about hull-blacking without which narrow-boat insurance is invalid. The A30 is audible at all times, and later in the day we'll walk up steep lanes known as stickle paths, which were responsible for the original A30 built in 1829; the stagecoaches couldn't get up and down the inclines. We have a similar problem, but if there's any ley energy to be sucked from the earth then Dru's blackthorn staff of power is yet to locate it.

If we want we can pause and think about our own lives as though they were ley lines, which are apparent alignments of mostly man-made landmarks

In the out-of-breath silences we have an incentive to prioritise the less-taxing metaphorical journey. If we want we can pause and think about our own lives as though they were ley lines, which are apparent alignments of mostly man-made landmarks. Looking back we can align one event with another in an attempt to find patterns and make sense of the past. This is the work that pilgrims can do, and if the ley lines fail to convince, then in retrospect life does look more like a labyrinth than a maze: we're old, and we know the path we took.

On an English pilgrimage, as Bunyan recognised, the metaphors are signposted in the place names. He invented Vanity Fair and By-Path

Meadow and the Slough of Despond. On our map, requiring no imagination at all, we have Yes Tor and Scarey Tor, Watchet Hill and Brat Tor. We spot the cluster of houses known as Good Frenchbeer.

'Meaning farm in Old English,' Dru says. 'Of course.'

The real advantage of calling our walk a pilgrimage is that we have a duty to look and learn. On a pilgrimage everything can become sacred in the same way that everything in an art gallery becomes art. Even the fire alarm is art, if that's the way you look at it, just as in nature the tortured stubborn roots of a beech tree can connect the natural and spiritual worlds – if that's how I choose to look at them. The Archangel's Way is spectacular with double meanings. White bracket fungi parasite chestnut trees, exoticizing them while at the same time killing them. Cherry trees are more beautiful in their blossom than in their fruit. The dappled hollow ways depend for their atmosphere on the past: filled to the brim with the melancholy of lost times yet still always hollow.

The path doesn't have its own official signposts, but an old marker for the Celtic Way leads us into a bog, the kind of tussocky wetland that has been bog since the beginning of time. We retreat, reflecting that the most common hubris of a pilgrimage (and therefore a life) is to think you know where you are. We accept our defeat with humility. We go backwards to go forwards, and the metaphors become exhausting, seeing one thing and looking for it to mean another.

We come down off the moor, metaphored-out, water bottle empty. In a house beside the road I see a woman washing up in the window. I wave a greeting and walk down the slope of the short drive towards her. She opens the window. Smart. I could be any old ruffian, so she doesn't want to risk the door. I hold up my bottle. She takes the bottle through the window and fills it from the tap. We chat; her name is Tracy and of course she knows the clergy who work on the moor. Who doesn't? I thank her and with my full water bottle I walk away, heart swelling with my benevolence at allowing Tracy to enact some Christian virtue. Then she comes out onto the road behind us. She calls us back and offers us coffee – people need time to think about being good.

As the kilometres pass the temperature drops and the shadows lengthen, until at the end of a day's walking the body becomes the centre of attention. A pilgrim is expected to suffer. Put a stone in your shoe and start for Jerusalem. Go barefoot from about Vienna onwards. Elect to camp on Dartmoor in early April in a tent that has seen better days.

The planned route of the Archangel's Way is rarely arduous, but we're carrying rucksacks and have a run of bad luck. In Tawton the church is closed, and so is the pub. It's like an early taste of English dystopia. Then at the Kings Arms in South Zeal they have an issue with the food. Or not the food exactly, which is imperishably in the deep freeze, but with a busted extractor fan when every

meal on the menu contains at least one fried item.
God is happy to make the middle classes suffer.

As the walking gets tougher (distance + time =
pain) we muse on how life could be improved. We
could find an abandoned bicycle, or even two. We
could come into possession of horses. We could live
in a house with a fire and not be on a pilgrimage
with a tent on our backs, but we've felt like this
before: on most of our walks we're pilgrims, a little
bit, because we like to play at Jesus. Be good, don't

> **We are day-tripping into a very mild form of
> sorrow. We're doing suffering in homeopathic
> quantities, which is enough to be going on with**

complain about the pain, and on Dartmoor keep
to Dru's suggested backing track of Arlo Guthrie's
Last Train to Glory: Arlo is not a man of constant
sorrow and he ain't seen trouble all day long. We
are day-tripping into a very mild form of sorrow.
We're doing suffering in homeopathic quantities,
which is enough to be going on with.

Wild camping is less a threat to civilization than
most people think. Dru and I share the feeling that
the locals won't mind as long as we leave in the
morning, which is usually our intention. We set up
the tent on a reclaimed slag heap near an old copper
mine, and the next day wake up with ice crisping
the flysheet. The second day is mostly off-moor, and
although Adrian suggested we might find ourselves
in our own way, the churches along the route give
us a nudge in case we need reminding that Jesus is

available. In the meantime we follow the traditional Christian advice for avoiding werewolves and the Devil himself: we stay on the path.

Most of the churches are open and hospitality is in evidence, with Please Enter written on gates and doors. The churches on the Archangel's Way offer the usual fascination of monogrammed porches, Restoration sundials, bosses of the Green Man and the three hares, granite fonts and decorated screens of casual antiquity. In the twenty-first century the church in Throwleigh hosts the Post Office, while at Sourton blue tits nest in the lectern, the holes at the front perfect facsimiles of a bird box. Churches along the route have co-opted standing stones and in Gidleigh a stream prettily dissects the graveyard.

Visiting old churches is not a sensationalist activity, and probably doesn't feature on many bucket lists. There's nothing here we'd go out of our way to see, but everything is interesting now we've come across it. We periodically take a break from everything in the world that is not the inside of a church, and it's no coincidence that the recurring words in the visitor books are beauty, peace, comfort. Thank you.

The Archangel's Way isn't the Camino, but it's cheaper and closer to home. The clergy who work on the moor hope that a walk like this can grow the rural church. Underused buildings can become rest stations for walkers, saving the churches for another few years from the withdrawn fate of The Old Post Office and The Old Rectory. The Old Church is not yet a common village address. When the Archangel's Way officially opens in 2020,

the churches might adapt with drying areas for walker's kit, or act as hubs for rent-a-tent schemes so that future pilgrims can travel light. There will be biscuits. The Dartmoor Camino may get its own stamped pilgrim passport, to be redeemed against discounted rates in local pubs and B&Bs — hospitality easily understood in terms of pounds and pence. Could that catch on? In each church a display board might suggest a self-improving task (imagine you're a tree), so that every stopping-point becomes an opportunity to engage spiritually in a new way with small acts of meditation and prayer.

Which would be great, I think, because metaphors in controlled doses are good for the understanding of the soul. If on this occasion Dru and I failed to find enlightenment, then we must have more roads ahead of us to travel, a metaphor that I imagine we'll be taking literally. ◼

by Antoinette Moses

Whose Play Is It Anyway?

If the Greeks invented tragedy, the Romans the epistle,
and the Renaissance the sonnet,
our generation invented a new literature,
that of testimony.
Elie Wiesel[1]

Just over ten years ago, I began to study and write verbatim or documentary theatre, a genre which creates its text from the theatrical realisation of original testimony and document. I wrote two plays, *Trash* and *Cuts*, that centred on the deaths of young women who had been in the care of the State. The words I used were those of their parents and, in the case of *Cuts*, those who spoke at an inquest into one such death. Previously I had drawn on texts to write fictionalised plays, such as one based on the encounter of El Greco and the Cardinal Fernando Niño de Guevara. I am currently writing a new play – *A Great Game* – that is a fictional reimagining of an international conference held at Evian-les-Bains in 1938, and which was called in response to the European refugee problem of the time. My play is a fiction that uses real people and events and some verbatim material.

In writing these plays, the question I constantly ask myself is: whose play is this? Am I acting as a mouthpiece for voices who would not otherwise be heard or be able to find an audience, or am I writing the play I want to write and using testimony simply as text?

Such questions are not new nor confined to fictional accounts of events. A recent article on the historian E.H. Carr, written by his great-grand-daughter Helen Carr, quotes his argument that history is written in the light of the social context of the writer and notes that facts 'are like fish on the fishmonger's slab. The historian collects them, takes them home and cooks and serves them.'[2]

Verbatim theatre follows a similar process. It promotes itself as a dramatisation of reality, but this stance prompts a number of questions in terms of its relationship with the real. Writing verbatim plays inevitably creates a tension between the creative impulse and a desire to honour both the words and the intention of those whose words the writer is using. Two parallel questions compete in the writer's head: to what extent does fidelity to the testimony limit the play or make it boring? And how can I be true to the testimony while at the same time write a play about specific issues? These being, in the first cases, women suffering from mental illness who are being imprisoned and, in my new play, the problem of individuals trying to find a solution to enforced mass migration.

David Hare has written several plays (*A Permanent Way*, *Stuff Happens* and *Via Dolorosa*) that have been called verbatim, although rarely by him. He has, however, said that these plays are 'a play like any other,'[3] and that they are crafted by him based on research in a similar way to his previous plays. But are they verbatim? The plays employ a mixture of testimony and record, but were either sourced from reported interviews which were not recorded (*The Permanent Way*) or blend recorded speeches with fiction (*Stuff Happens*). Hare is not alone; Tanika Gupta also mixes testimony and fiction in *Gladiator*

However, if audiences watch these plays in the expectation of being witnesses to a representation of reality, then the blurring of the actual with the fictional does raise questions of authenticity and authorship

Games. However, if audiences watch these plays in the expectation of being witnesses to a representation of reality, then the blurring of the actual with the fictional does raise questions of authenticity and authorship. In recent years, academics have argued that plays that appear to be documentary should be strictly verbatim (as many are) while others argue that what is most important is the intentionality of the original speakers. This latter, unsurprisingly, is generally assumed by the playwright.

One of the pioneers of documentary theatre, Emily Mann, has described the process of writing such plays as: going out to find the event, going to the place, researching and interviewing, and then constructing the play from life. 'It's very personal,' she writes[4]. But is it personal in terms of exploring – some might say exploiting – the lives of others, or personal to the playwright?

In creating *Cuts* and *Trash*, I wanted to write a play about how women with severe mental problems were ending up in English prisons because the mental health services had refused to help them. In one of the inquest scenes in *Cuts*, the expert witness, one of Britain's leading psychologists, makes this point forcefully. Thus I began with a thesis and needed real people to embody it.

I found them at a rally for the United Friends and Families Campaign at Trafalgar Square on Saturday 28th October 2006. Here, I met a number of parents and siblings of women who had died in prison or in the care of the State. These included Jean Pearson, the protagonist of *Trash*, and Kirsty Blanksby, the sister of Petra Blanksby, who had killed herself in prison having been imprisoned for trying to kill herself. Petra became the protagonist of *Cuts*. I also talked to Pauline Campbell, whose daughter, Sarah, had died in Styal and who I had previously met when I attended one of her prison demonstrations at Eastwood Park. It was evident that there were extremely sad personal stories behind each of the deaths. My decision of whose story would be told, however, would depend not only on the character of the deceased and on their family's willingness to allow their story to become a play, but on the inherent value of the individual narrative as part of the overall story I wished to tell. I was therefore creating my story by editing out any people whose narrative did not fit my case.*

* Pauline Campbell, sadly, committed suicide while I was researching the play and I did not feel it appropriate, therefore, to include any scene that might be critical of her.

The rally, while it provided me with the necessary contacts, also highlighted the aleatory nature of writing a verbatim play that is not based on a specific event or person. The choice of story and characters was very much a matter of chance. Furthermore, my first contact with the families left me with a sense of ambivalence and serious doubts as to whether I could write these plays. One concern was that the reasons for the families to tell their stories were not the same as the reason I wanted to write the plays, although there were areas of consensus. In most cases, the families wanted to apportion blame, while I wanted to widen the story. Moreover, those who attended the rally were self-selecting in that these were the families who were campaigning for justice. There were many other stories of women who had also died in prison, which would not be told because their families preferred to grieve in private.

Nevertheless, I followed up the contacts made at the rally. Interviewing Jean, I found the story that would become *Trash*, and Pauline Campbell put me in touch with Pete Blanksby, Petra's father. From that moment, the authorship of both *Trash* and *Cuts* moved from my control over the text to a negotiated control between myself and the families of the young women who died. They didn't ask me to make any major changes − except for one line about Kelly that Jean asked me to cut because she felt it was too personal − but that the text of the stories was now also controlled by those who had lived them.

Trash and *Cuts* do represent my point of view. I exercised control over these stories through the way the texts were edited, and in the structure of the plays. Jean Pearson wanted to tell the story of her daughter's death and assign blame. I wrote a play

In my work-in-progress ... the parallels with today are what interest me most: the threat of fascism and how the world is failing to respond to an international refugee crisis

that shows how a mother changed by having to deal with her daughter's death. The change also allowed the audience to observe Jean in a more critical fashion and become aware that she might not be the most reliable witness. I chose not to add any testimony that contradicted Jean's version of events, nor did I follow up other sources for their version of the story. I knew from what Jean herself said that her version would be contradicted by others, and that how she saw herself was not the same as how she was seen by those with whom she came into conflict. My aim was not to create a naturalistic drama of oppositions, but to allow the audience the freedom to observe and evaluate Jean from their own interpretation of her words.

In my work-in-progress, concerning the conference at Evian, the parallels with today are what interest me most: the threat of fascism and how the world is failing to respond to an international refugee crisis. These are the same issues that concern my characters, but the dialogue I have given them is almost certainly more overt than the way in which they would have spoken at the time. Much of the play is supposition based on known facts (there are telegrams to Roosevelt from the Conference chairman, Myron Taylor and a verbatim record of the Conference speeches)[5] but these were mostly used as research not as material. However, I do include extracts from Victor Cazalet's letter to The Times, and from a speech to the House of Commons. The first comes from a biography of Cazalet[6], the second from Hansard. The fictional retelling of the Jewish refugees on the tugboat in the Danube is based on several sources including contemporaneous articles in *The Jewish Telegraph Agency* and a report at the time by Maria Schmolka now in the Archives of the Czech Republic[7]. I took these speeches and reports as permission to use them as dialogue. Unlike Truman Capote, who eschewed the tape recorder and, according to his friend Harper Lee, had 'long ago put fact out of business,' I use the actual words of my characters whenever I can.

Helen Carr, in her piece on her great grandfather, also notes that he believed the job of anyone writing about the past was 'a continuous process of interaction between the historian and his facts, an unending dialogue between the present and the past.'[8] You could say the same of verbatim theatre. ▉

[1] Elie Wiesel. 'The Holocaust as Inspiration.' *Dimensions of the Holocaust: Lectures at Northwestern University*, edited by E. Wiesel, L. Dawidowicz, D. Rabinowitz and M. McAfee Brown. Evanston, IL, Northwestern University Press, 1977, p9.

[2] Helen Carr. 'History According to EH Carr.' *New Statesman*, 8th May 2019

[3] David Hare. *Obedience, Struggle and Revolt*. London: Faber, 2005, p78.

[4] Gary Dawson. *Documentary Theatre in the United States: An Historical Survey and Analysis of its Content, Form and Stagecraft*. Santa Barbara, CA: Praeger, 1999, p5.

[5] Proceedings of the Intergovernmental Committee July 6 to 15th 1938 Verbatim Record of the plenary meetings, resolutions and reports

[6] Cited in the partisan and heavily censored biography of Cazalet by the Conservative politician, Richard Rhodes James, 1976.

[7] Michal Frankl. 'Reports from the No-Man's-Land.' *EHRI Document Blog*. 19 January 2016. https://blog.ehri-project.eu/2016/01/19/reports-from-the-no-mans-land/

[8] Helen Carr.

A Great Game

*Extract from an early draft of a play based on the
1938 Conference at Evian-les-Bains by Antoinette Moses*

Act 1

Sunday 3rd July, Royal Hotel, Evian-les-Bains, France and
then into chorus as 1948.

Setting the stage for the Conference. This could be setting
out tables, organising papers, waiters and hotel staff
preparing.

And we hear the sound of the hotel orchestra tuning up or
practising some of the hits of the year such as Boum! by
Charles Trenet.

The sense of bustle and purpose could begin even as the
audience are taking their seats. This sets the tone for the
energy of the play which should flow quickly from scene to
scene. The cast who are included in the bustle begin to shape
into a chorus and assume their characters. All are present
except Heinrich. For accents see their later entrances.

JAMES   Evian. *(Sighs)* We had such high hopes.

ROGER   You had such high hopes.

JAMES   You never wanted the Conference to take
place.

ROGER   Was I wrong?

JANOS   We all hoped. None more than Victor.

VICTOR   This was the moment for something concrete.

JAMES   Victor'd been calling for something to happen. That letter you wrote to the British Times.

VICTOR   In May?

James nods.

VICTOR   I was so angry. I couldn't believe. I *(takes a deep breath)*

Dear Sir, It is inconceivable the world can look on much longer and see what amounts to the extermination of the European Jews without finding among the empty spaces of the earth some asylum for them.

ROGER   You said what no one else was prepared to say then.

ROBIN   So many people think the extermination of the European Jews wasn't even considered before the War.

MARY   People forget. In any case nobody took such warnings seriously. (Beat) Nobody took Victor seriously. Sorry, Victor, but it's true.

VICTOR   I was something of a Jeremiah. *(Beat)* But
            Evian. Evian was going to be where we'd find
            a home for the refugees.

JANOS   Now when we look back…

ROBIN   When you look back what do you remember,
            Janos?

JANOS   Many things, Robin, my dear. Many things.

TIMOTHY   It's all right for you, Janos. After the war, you
            married the richest heiress in America.

JANOS   One of the richest.

TIMOTHY   Now you're back in Germany with US money
            and control a portfolio of eighteen newspapers.

JANOS   With my new pretty actress wife, except we're
            getting divorced; I happen to have fallen in
            love again. Darling Eloise.

TIMOTHY   About to shed the fifth of six wives, not to
            mention the mistresses…

JANOS   Is it my fault women love me?

            I thought this was about Evian. Evian made me
            a soldier, did you know that? I joined the French
            Foreign Legion. We were captured. I escaped.

JAMES	And turned the story into a novel.
TIMOTHY	Which became a film.
JANOS	With Gene Kelly and Peter Lorre. It was nothing like my novel. A travesty. My novel was superb. And I will go on to write twenty-five novels and over ten thousand articles. /
ROGER	/Your energy exhausts me.
ROBIN	Only matched by your self-regard. Don't look at me like that, Janos. It's hardly news, even to yourself.
JANOS	And you went back to Europe as a war correspondent, Robin. Where we lost you. But then even at Evian/
ROBIN	/It all comes back to Evian.
MARY	That was the moment I knew… I just knew that the time was over for the old ruling class. We had to create change in Britain. And we have. A socialist Government. The Welfare State.
VICTOR	I don't believe Britain understands socialism. Those who espouse the cause have never influenced the upper or governing class in England. It's a class to which the people rally in times of need. It won the war.

MARY	And was promptly ejected by the people.
ROGER	Not for very long I think.
JAMES	I think of Evian as a failure of humanity.
ROGER	It was never intended to achieve anything. Think of whom they put in charge.
VICTOR	Winterton. Stupid, short-sighted, bigoted politician. He only cared about keeping the British Colonies out of the discussions.
JAMES	But it was your Prime Minister who sent the Colonial Office to Evian. Roger Makins was the lone Foreign Office chap there.

Roger nods assent.

VICTOR	As soon as I saw that I began to worry. Even before the Conference began Winterton did a deal with the Americans to ensure Palestine was off the table. I tried to intervene.
JAMES	You have to admit that Victor tried. And I tried. Myron Taylor wouldn't

listen to me. He was Roosevelt's man through and through. Victor said what we all thought.

TIMOTHY   That was Victor. He told me to go to the mountains. He said that's where I'd be most useful. He died so young.

MARY   We were all young in Evian. Even those of us who weren't.

JAMES   We'll never forget those few days in July.

MARY   *(Looks towards Robin)* And the friends we made.

ROBIN   *(Looks towards Janos)* And the friends we lost.

For me it didn't begin in Evian. It began in Czechoslovakia. Sunday 3rd July. I'm in a shabby hotel. It's a hot afternoon.

And cast exit, apart from Robin, Janos and Timothy as we move to Bratislava.

ROBIN, 35, an American journalist, edits her copy from her typed notes. She wears linen trousers and a loose cotton sweater and the makeup of the period. On a small table beside her is an ashtray and a glass of whisky. There is also a battered leather holdall beside her and a typewriter box case. Voice is East Coast.

ROBIN   *(Reads)* I am writing to you today from Bratislava, a city in Eastern Europe where the borders of Austria, Czechoslovakia and Hungary meet. *(Stops reading)* Bit clunky. Where many borders meet?

       (Reads) An early mist rises off the River Danube, and to my right, the four towers of the castle are just visible in the distance. Two swans drift by as if to underline the beauty of this scene.

She stops reading, grimaces at the exaggeration of the writing and takes a swig of the whisky.

       Well, they might have done. Get on with it, woman. Tell the story.

She takes out a cigarette, lights it and takes a puff, then puts it into the ashtray.

ROBIN   So where was I? *(Reads)* However, I am not here to admire the view, but to bring you the tragic news of the sixty-one men, women and children who are incarcerated on an ancient tugboat moored a few miles upstream in this fast-flowing current.

Let me tell you their story, a strange game of international ping pong.

Stops reading.

Yeah. I like that.

(Reads) One night in April, Austrian police arrived at a small town near the border, and several truckloads of Jews were forced from their homes and taken by boat across the river to Czechoslovakia. Here, the local people gave them some food and assistance… *(Stops reading)* Maybe 'eventually'.

(Reads) Here the local people eventually gave them some food and assistance and returned them to their country of origin. The Austrians repeated this performance with Hungary, but here again they were not granted admission.

For the next three days and nights, they were abandoned on a narrow strip of no-man's-land. It was a bitterly cold Spring and they had no food or shelter.

Finally, a few kind people found them a dilapidated boat on which they could temporarily stay. And that is where they have been for the past eight weeks.

She stops reading, swigs her drink and one of the sheets of paper falls to the ground.

Where am I now? Here we are. *(Reads)* For the past eight weeks, moored on the river, half in Hungary, half in Czechoslovakia. When I managed to visit them yesterday, I found unspeakable misery.

Her voice changes. She's back there with them.

Picture the scene if you will. The deck is so small they cannot sit on it together, so they have to stand for much of the day or go below decks where it's filthy, swarming with rats.

She takes another swig.

Rachel, a mother with three children under eight, told me that the rats are the worst problem. Each night the women take turns to stay

awake, to safeguard their infants and
prevent them from being bitten.

I was a dressmaker, she tells me.
I specialised in embroidery, you
should have seen some of my dresses.
She broke off. Our families have
lived in Austria for generations, she
says. Now we have no home. The
children try not to cry, but it is so
hard on them.

Rachel and her companions wish
only to protect their own families
and live decent lives in a new
country. Today their hopes rest on
the decisions made at the Evian
Conference on Refugees which will
open in two days' time, on July 5th.
The conscience of the world will
move for a few days to France, where
thirty-two nations come together
to bring hope to the thousands like
Rachel who now find themselves
without a nation.

Today for the sake of for those on the
tug boat and all those throughout
Germany and Austria, we pray that
a resolution is found to bring an end
to this suffering.

Stops reading, puts down the paper and begins to pack up her stuff.

Yeah. I pray, you pray, we all pray. Will anything happen? Who knows? *(Beat)* Okeydokey. Let's send this off and go to Evian, wherever the hell that is. On some Swiss lake. Only it's in France. They do go in for borders, these Europeans, you never know where the fuck you are.

And so we press on. God help us all.

Packs away her typewriter, throws her cigarettes and bottle of whisky into her bag, picks up her stuff and exits.

ROBIN (O/S) Auschecken, check out, bitte.

2019
PRINTMAKING
COURSES
&
ACTIVITIES

Print to the People are dedicated to promotion of traditional printmaking processes, providing a range of activities for all levels of experience. All activities take place at our new studios:

The Box Factory
53-55 Pitt St,
Anglia Square, Norwich,
NR3 1DE.

For the full list of courses and activities, including dates, times and how to book please visit our website below:

- **SCREEN PRINTING**
- **LINO CUT**
- **LETTERPRESS**
- **ETCHING**
- **RISOGRAPH**
- **HAND DRAWN TYPE**
- **TEXTILE CYANOTYPE**

PROMOTING TRADITIONAL PRINTMAKING PROCESSES
PRINT TO THE PEOPLE

WWW.PRINTTOTHEPEOPLE.COM

For my grandmother, my mother and my sisters

On Krakowskie

by Kinga Elwira Cybulska

Przedmieście

2007, From Lublin With Love

'Congestive heart failure,' my mother said. Granny had called her Dana and Dana called me to pronounce the direct cause of death. The sour milk of morning clouded my weak eyes.

1921, Lublin

The life of Stasia Jońska opens for me at the age of eight, when her mother Marjanna married for the second time. Stanisław Matusiak, who had been a husband before (to a woman 15 years older), now became a 'father figure' to a vast collection of children. Indeed, the gift of babies had come often to the family, irresistible to refuse. Only Stasia, the last to be born and the last to die, would remember them all.

There was Jerzyk Joński who had soup delivered to the hospital regularly. An eternal bachelor, whose life was spent mixing water and rye, who knew dawn like the inside of his pockets.

There was Mietek Joński. A butcher with a sharp tongue.

Kazia Jońska. A vague black branch of the genealogy. A broken tree.

Zygmunt Joński journeyed to War-szawa... War-szawa... War-szawa...

Zofja Jońska died aged eighteen.

Janka Jońska and her two tiny girls. One would overuse stomach acid relief and develop Alzheimer's. The other would be proud of her children and die alone in the hallway of an overcrowded hospital.

Lasieńka Jońska, the beloved sister. Stasia would rock her strong baby boys as if they were her own, a prelude to motherhood. Did they remember the aunt who had changed their cotton nappies and secured them with pins? Lives cut short, little time to forget. Lasieńka went to the photographer at Krakowskie Przedmieście to fix her life in sepia, an eternal memory. The rounded edges. The face elongated.

Born so late, Stasia Ewa Jońska; never learnt to cycle, never spoke French with a Frenchman, never had a pet.

—

Krótka Street, Number 3, Flat 25. The patched-up family received a bargain of a life cherished above all. With an occasional glimpse into an obscure future. Up the street, a travel agency selling promises, tickets to America – golden dreams. Stasia would pass it regularly. 'Lot' means flight and this was the only Polish airline cutting through the Iron Curtain. The Joński/Jońska children would only make it to Warszawa or Poznań.

And some sanatorium where the female patients
were complemented by cardiac patients, geriatric
men. Pale food was served in a canteen and
entertainment on sickly evenings. They took delight
in postcards from friends scattered around different
parts of the new Poland.

———

At times the powdered light of morning exposed
the high creature of creatures. Initially, a god of
minor things. Jewish bagels sold on many corners
of Krakowskie Przedmieście. Soft and round.
Mastered by Hersz Lender in Lublin.[1] Lender
turned out to be lucky. New York welcomed his
breakfast creations. Sad as poppy seeds and light as
sesame. And there was soda water with juice which
everyone drank from one glass. A glass was wiped,
likewise tender stomachs. And more bagels shared
with siblings.

When still a child and before medical predicaments, Stasia ate too much sugar and confessed. Poison for the teeth from the rotted West

When still a child and before medical
predicaments, Stasia ate too much sugar and
confessed. Poison for the teeth from the rotted
West. She had reached the age of preparation for
becoming part of the ephemeral body of god. She
would have preferred a goddess. The taste could
have been sweeter. 'Is gluttony the new season for

you? Kneel down and beg for forgiveness. You are a bad, bad girl'. She pretended to kiss the rustling purple and gold robe and left with her hands buried in the pockets of an old coat inherited from her big sister Lasieńka. The Lacrimosa of household poverty.

1931-1945, Lublin

The Order of the Holy Ghost nuns came to Lublin in 1922 and founded a private Catholic school for girls[2] with an honourable mission: to educate the poor and unprivileged who lived in unheated flats with few dreams and aspirations. The Messiah was tucked between the narrow streets of Old Town. Stasia found her way here each day.

She walked along Krakowskie Przedmieście, churches on the right-hand side (ink-wounded fingers clutched at some notebooks tied with a strap) and churches on the left-hand side (her young heart would not remember much yet), sheltering in the half circle of the Krakowska Gate, which descended into the school building filled with whispers and shades. Wearing a modest uniform, Stasia appeared younger than she was. The pupils were told to sit, revise and pray. All three in changing order. Some failed trust for teachers and life resulted in two unsatisfactory marks in the first grade: mathematics and history. Swallowing her pride and applying herself, a satisfactory mark in French followed; Stasia mastered 'Comme si, comme sa'.

The older sister was still there for her; Lasieńka, separated by just two years in age, but an ocean of experience, expectations and prospects, was still there for her. In the autumn of 1934, a candidate for marriage appeared and the girl with the

> **Stasia ventured east, to Hrubieszów to be close to her sibling, rocking the babies that were born as Lublin began to fill with ashes, rubble and a sour odour**

elongated face became a wife and, soon after, a mother. Stasia, on receiving her 'matura' certificate (marks for very good behaviour, physical exercise, and hygiene), became an aunt, now proficient in cooking, sewing and cleaning. They had not taught Stasia about babies at the Catholic school. But Stasia ventured east, to Hrubieszów – a piece of Roman Catholic, Greek Catholic and Jewish land – to be close to her sibling, rocking the babies that were born as Lublin began to fill with ashes, rubble and a sour odour. A hint of angels and the murk of the unknown.

––

And so the tremendous unknown morphed into the visible. 1939. Aeroplanes, aeroplanes; a sinister buzzing, blackening and the cruelty of progress.

Chopin Street, with its ornaments of secession visible from Krakowskie Przedmieście, and which Stasia had passed so many times, was now carved and cut. Chopin buried under flying debris. A musical prelude to blackness poured from broken windows. Ears perforated by steel and blood wished they were deaf. People grew eyes like deer. The tenderness of exposed flesh. The pandemonium of misfortune.

—

1939. Krakowskie Przedmieście, Narutowicza, Kapucyńska, Kościuszki, Chopina, Bramowa: all were now moveable targets for the Luftwaffe.

When they were young they played at killing. Friends died and rose again; repeat, repeat, repeat. As they grew up others convinced them to play some more, with teeth grinding and fists clenched on control panels, tearing buildings and bodies. Boys played at killing while girls bandaged wounds; two sides of the war story.

An early casualty was Józef Czechowicz, Lublin's only famous poet. Killed while he was at the barbers, a Polish-German dictionary tucked in his pocket. Tufts of hair, brittle pages and the roar of aeroplanes overhead.

The Town Hall was a favourite target. The hum of rustling Polish was about to be silenced when the cleaner Jan Gilas hurried outside and fell, curled like an embryo, clutching a bomb nearly half his size and weighing around 50 kilograms. He had carried it out of the crowded building on pay day as many queued. The bomb never detonated, but it made Jan's heart stop beating.[3]

1945, Warszawa
The May victory of 1945 turned promptly into a

defeat of another kind. The war was all over. Was it over? The Red Army 'liberated' us...

But on 17th October 1945 the capital of the new socialist-realist Poland acquired a very precious heart. This heart would be returned to the pillar of the Church of the Holy Cross on Krakowskie Przedmieście. Chopin's body was buried in Paris, at the Père Lachaise cemetery, but his heart was kept by a sister and smuggled back into Poland in 1850. Stilled life nested in a jar. Bigger than usual, it had already been imprisoned for 39 years in the fragile cage of Chopin's ribs. As there are always two sides of the story, it is not established who guarded the heart later; whether the barbarian Nazis known also for their taste in classical music or the National Army soldiers protecting the symbol of distant romanticism. The swollen human paraphernalia was sacred. Warszawa with its broken ribs of buildings and a firm voice of the new Polish Radio reporter:

'Warszawa is experiencing sublime moments. The heart of our great artist is returning now to the capital'.[4]

1945-1947, Lublin
152 kilometres from Warszawa, should one draw a straight, imaginary line on the map, which changed so many times people did not know whether any order would prove temporary or final. A train would take its time, as if reluctant to pull itself out of this one-star town, a town on the eastern border that had been punished severely and was now on its way

to a doubtful recovery. Here April snow mingled
with bloodless dirt, clotting Stasia's clothing.
Nightmares still came, teeth felt like silent stones
that Stasia fought to spit out. Relief never arrived.

The maternal shape of the hotel bore a balcony.
Once Grand, then Deutsches Haus, and now Bar
Centralny on Krakowskie Przedmieście,[5] offering
vodka shots, grey pieces of herring curled like
oppressed tongues and 'cold legs', pork leftovers
drowned mercilessly in dull jelly. Delicacies of
the new, coward's world. At intervals, Stasia was
mourning it, but something else burdened her mind.

She had been there almost an hour, recalling
forgotten French words: 'C'est la vie, comme si,
comme ca'.

Pale, dry lips and dark hair elegantly pinned up
by her own steady hand. A protest in a place where
any form of difference was unwelcome. 'C'est la vie,
comme si, comme ca,' interspersed with a mastery
of gastric ventriloquism. For breakfast, she had one
piece of rye bread layered with sweaty lard. For
dinner the cookery book advised ingenious recipes:

Fish soup without fish:
60 grams of potatoes
2 big onions
4 peppercorns
1 bay leaf
salt
optionally: a glass of milk or 10 ml of cream.

Peel potatoes and cut into squares. Cut the
onions and cook in 1 and ½ litre of water adding
crushed peppercorns and a leaf. Add potatoes and
cook. Serve immediately. The soup is not that
different in flavour from the fish broth.[6]

Working at an office, where dark hours of the new
Poland were devoted to bookkeeping (and siphoning
scraps off unfortunate, vulnerable people), Stasia
persisted. Izba Skarbowa[7] was a neat building, shelved
with records, precisely kept, in which Stasia's pre-war
education paid off. She walked once again the same
route as years before, every day through Krakowskie
Przedmieście, which was waking up slowly, concealing
its bruises and open concrete wounds. The Jewish bagels
Stasia had been raised on were replaced with things
to come, black mouths of destroyed shops needed to
be stoppered urgently. But strengthened by meticulous
working-through-the-numbers, she chose to continue.
     One cannot underestimate the convenience
of neutral mathematics, its provision of safety; a
luxury for others. Office work came with a price at
times – Stasia bit her mother tongue while listening to
colleagues, those mannequins of decent beings. In a
cold, musty washroom she rinsed ink from her fingers
and comforted another girl; encouraged her to resist
the demons of male harassment. The girl was losing
this crude game, but Stasia could talk back.
     She was winning. Anywhere. Anytime. Teeth
would not break like stones. The office chit-chat of
villagers forced to move to towns could not hurt. So
many escapes to the unknown; so many times had

she witnessed instincts worse than those of animals. No job could imprison. What could imprison Stasia more than the constant need to help others, to fight for food and coal, then fight some more?

This short, fragile, dignified man whose eyes fed on a black diet of poor ink, failed to notice his woman at first, the smile drawing slowly across her face

She still did not have a room of her own. Girls the shape of Stasia could bear it easily. Girls of Stasia's spirit would never break, they would always find a solution. At least there was no longer a need to wash the monthly impurity from her cheap work clothes. Instead, the waist was altered, secretly let out in the morning before nausea licked her throat.

Bones felt like they were made of chalk, and the weather's rawness would crush them before the man she was waiting for would arrive at Bar Centralny. Its neon shone with the dull light of an economic system, offering modern life to the tormented. This short, fragile, dignified man whose eyes fed on a black diet of poor ink, failed to notice his woman at first, the smile drawing slowly across her face. Hot glasses filled with weak tea that danced softly against the crudeness of a waitress. He approached the table, took her hands, gently kissed the fingertips with their traces of grey laundry soap and whispered (with an inconspicuous exclamation mark):

'I've got the place, dear. I did exactly what you told me to do.'

Soon, they were both drowning in a silvery evening. On their way to their first home.

1982, Lublin

The new Poland sunk in the lurid summer. Dust
swirled inside the red trolley buses cutting through
Krakowskie Przedmieście and settled on seats
that bore the tired souls of an internal and eternal
polityka. Two women hurried to the taxi rank.

'You'll make it!' Stasia always accepted things the
way they were and got on with them promptly. It
had started, they both knew.

'To the hospital...'

New Poland crawled on scabby knees after the
war Stasia had experienced, but Dana did not yet
know that in the maternity ward there was constant
conflict of another kind, a secret pact of midwives
against frail ballooned bodies. A burgundy, livid,
jaundiced slaughterhouse, not for the innocent – they
all deserved what they were getting, the staff was
convinced. No mercy, had they failed to cooperate
or to devote their bodies, stretched like rosy jellyfish
for the noble cause. When everything was rationed,
including decency, the whole system depended on a
suspicious state. The national attribute– 'Polishness'
– was pushed out of the female bodies with great
effort. Dana was in the splattered vacuum with
her mother on the other side. There was nothing
even Stasia could do, except wag her finger at a
sulky midwife and fail to make her see sense.
Dana thought why would one waste time?

The nurses were further agitated by the busy doctor
in a non-iron fluorescent RFN shirt (a gift from the

grateful director of a meat factory), who had to be bothered to perform an operation on one of the women. The midwives' tireless faces, cheap powder between the premature wrinkles, stretched as they ranted.

'Don't you have any milk?... You've got more than you think... Your fault... Bad attitude... Didn't you manage to push out the baby... Caesarean section for the lazy ones... Well, not real women...Did you make that noise with a man... Hysterical drama queen...'

So Dana became one of the Polish queens and did not dare to admit she was a trainee doctor herself. All the women in her family gripped their luscious dark hair and pulled it, transferring the pain to the roots of organic matter. Dana's own curls were pulled back and secured with a lilac polyester band for the sake of inheritance of gestures. Every sip of stewed raspberry drink ('kompot') scolded her dry lips.

Stasia did not approve of cosmetics, hard work cutting through your skin was something to be proud of!

Forced to wear the obligatory birth uniform (too short and too coarse, like a dead animal fur on which she placed her royal-blue-boxed Nivea-scented hands), Dana thought of her mother giving birth – when all you could do was to get over it, because that was your unquestionable duty, to produce another citizen of the scarred country. Stasia did not approve of cosmetics, hard work cutting through your skin was something to be proud of! Dana's father would say: 'I don't wish to interfere...'

(At this particular moment, Dana's intellect is turning to mud and her heart to a pulp, she is a corpse stuffed with black froth and white cotton balls. A lesson from her pathology classes.)

On her back, in her loneliness, like her mother. Dying was easy. She was hollow.

'It's a girl!'

She was yet to discover the infant would smell like sour pineapple, had she the opportunity to sample this fruit from behind the iron curtain of ruthless economic rules.

For now, Dana survived, but it was not over. After Stasia discharged her from the State Maternity Hospital, Lubartowska Street, her daughter felt an unexpected cramp in her tender belly. Stasia's words jingled in the air:

'What I've told you? C'est la vie, my child'.

Dana's father carried her new flesh and bone, her darling baby. Dana stopped, still protected by his vulnerable arm and bad eyes. She looked down. Shoes were filled with blood and the concrete pavement was blossoming like poppies.

1984, Lublin

I am two and I stick a finger in my newborn sister's eye. She is a baby doll and I am a doll and my granny's hands bleed with beetroot; she is peeling it for soup and the scream makes her run out of the kitchen. She smacks me ('You little hooligan!') with a wet tea towel, so I will remember that I have done wrong. I see knives of light.

1990, Lublin

They tell me I stuck a finger in my little sister's eye.

Someone has opened a new shop. 'Delicatessen', it is called. This is the first time I see shrimps. Fat fingers resting on the blocks of ice. This is the first time after Pewex[8] that a shop can stock so many wonderful things. A carton of juice with a straw, how ingenious! And Kouou Roukou, a wafer with cocoa and Donald Duck bubble gum. Mum doesn't like it when I stick it to the desk that I share with my sister. Mum likes our room tidy. And we cannot touch our face with our hands. And our hair neat, no tangles allowed.

All our friends have a dad. We have each other.

I love jigsaw puzzles. I spend a lot of time matching all the pieces up. I don't like it when I can't find a piece. It upsets me.

My granny says 'No need to cry, my child, you'll cry when your mother dies, not now!'

And I guess she's right. The carpet is stiff and hurts my knees. I look at them and see a flower which looks like a flower on a carpet.

1994, Lublin

My grandmother's fingers are dirty with the first cherries' juice. She uses a safety pin to get to the stone heart. 'Stuk, stuk' dropped into a ceramic bowl with zigzags of red. It takes a lot of time. Mum doesn't have this time. She wanted to be a heart doctor, but she has us.

My grandmother also makes the best pickles: peppers, zucchini (which she says is Italian and I think it is a bit like cucumber, but better). They have a lot of vitamins for strong bones and good eye-sight. Summers are short and she is always busy in the kitchen. Winter is coming and winters

My grandmother's fingers are dirty with the first cherries' juice. She uses a safety pin to get to the stone heart. 'Stuk, stuk' dropped into a ceramic bowl with zigzags of red'

here can be as annoying as flu. So we play games: countries, cities, animals, colours. We learn new words: list as many words as you can starting with a particular letter of the alphabet. We've got only five minutes. 'B' is for a brush (she often brushes my long messy hair) and for babcia, granny.

1997, Lublin
Our muddled eyes. We go together with my granny for eye appointments. We walk cutting through Krakowskie Przedmieście. My school route. I hold her arm, she seems apprehensive of the cars – before the war there were never so many cars in Lublin. Churches however, stand firm. I count them.

We enter the waiting room first (someone's wet fur that smells disgustingly of mothballs). Meat disgusts me, too. My mother never cooks pork. Pork smells human, like a corpse. She says it is because pigs' blood resembles our blood, their organs work like our organs. Pigs adjust to different environments, they can be trained; but once something snaps, they will go back to their old habits. Just like us. I believe if you eat pork, you eat a pig's fear. That's why I gag when I smell it. I would throw up fear as fast as I can. Fear also feeds on the sweets that I desire. And it manifests when I need to speak to people. My granny does not understand it.

Inside the stuffy waiting room Stasia talks to everyone. About her physical condition, her son in America and, finally, her war. An old man has been waiting for hours. Murmuring to himself (his daughter glued to the chair and her own thoughts), he calls divine names and whistles with a shortness of breath.

'Are they going to see me at all, I've heard one can destroy this part of an eye by looking at the sunlight, hahaha, I was hanging out in the sewers, who was staring at the sun?'

2006, Lublin

This is the last time I see her. She is still able to stand on her own. I grew on fruit-filled dumplings and tangy vegetables and now I am taller than her. A papier-mâché of a granny pressed against the high ceramic stove (installed in an attempt to heat spacious apartments in the early 20th century). We used to throw our milk teeth behind it, I wondered whether they were still stored there. There was no Tooth Fairy in Poland.

In the morning I help her to bathe. There is only one thing she requests help with. She asks me to scrub her back.

'Harder!' she shouts. The skin is dry, with discolouration in the form of tiny islands. A memory of sun and time. 'Harder, harder, girl!' the brush presses firmer and firmer. She is becoming a curled form rooted in this old bath with its black plague of cracks.

But now, now she is standing against the high stove. Arms folded, she wears a cardigan. She is so cold. It is so brown. Colour of fermented amber. Matching her watercolour eyes, her once-chestnut eyes.

My sister says the cardigan was blue.

2007, Lublin

You had some rehearsals of which I am aware. Running away from the Ukrainian Insurgent Army (UPA) soldiers: 'What's the rush for, miss?' And 'Get away from the hospital, the Nazis are throwing newborns out of the window!' Lubartowska Street cracked. Respectively: two childbirths, one stomach perforation.

Hearing goes first, but it is also the first to come back. You would recognise Chopin and forget Chopin. There are no familiar voices around you, but how do you define familiar when you are fading? On your night table: a cotton handkerchief and the prune juice provided by your absent son. You check obsessively whether you have enough bread and toilet paper.

There are no familiar faces. Sisters and granddaughters, they all merge into one. You no longer remember. I wish I had asked you about many things, but youth has its own ignorance.

You have short, dark hair with touches of white.

You suffer from bulging veins and wear thick stockings. Your fingers, resembling tiny branches of an extraordinary tree, are clutching a blanket.

But the frozen cocoon of a bed swallows you whole.

2017, various locations
When you were my age you married and had your first child growing under your heart. Classical music calms babies suspended in the invisible underwater; and you could have been listening to piano strokes and rocking to nocturnes with your swollen body and remembering the Polonaise from your school graduation ball before it was too dangerous to perform Chopin's music.

Hearing goes first, but it is also the first to come back. You would recognise Chopin and forget Chopin

It is impossible to understand this tormented Central European country without Chopin. The admiration was so intense that we cherished his precious heart, preserved in a jar, human remains pickled. Two lives, as any immigrant's life doubles, one heart, and many speculations on the cause of death (cystic fibrosis among others). The crystal jar filled with cognac did not open. The floating organ appeared yellowish, as if worn out and aged, unknown *terra* of fortunes and misfortunes. It was so efficiently preserved that thorough observations (taken by a medical team under Professor Tadeusz Dobosz) established the ultimate diagnosis: tuberculosis compromised the heart muscles.[9] When a weakened composer and a great aesthete was fading, he kept saying 'Swear to make them cut me open, so I won't be buried alive.'[10]

Stasia used to announce: 'Make them burn my body, so I won't be eaten by worms!' She is now resting in an uncertain place. Mostly in my recurring dreams. ∎

[1] T. Pietrasiewicz, (2014). Esej o bajglach i cebularzach. Retrieved 1 November 2017 from http://www.jemlublin.pl/tomasz-pietrasiewicz-esej-o-cebularzach/

[2] Rybicka, (2013). Historia VIII LO. Retrieved 15 November, 2017 from http:/lo8.lublin.pl/content/historia-viii-lo

[3] W. Białasiewicz, A.L. Gzella, Bronili Lublina. Wrzesień 1939, Lublin,1994, p44.

[4] Śmierciak, K.. Trudne losy serca Chopina. Przyjechało w słoiku, 20 lat przeleżało w rupieciarni. 17 September 2014. Accessed 1 December 1 2017, from https://tvnwarszawa.tvn24.pl/informacje,news,trudne-losy-serca-chopina-przyjechalobr-w-sloiku-20-lat-lezalo-w-rupieciarni,142718.html

[5] Polskie Radio. Fryderyk Chopin: Zabierzcie przynajmniej serce me do Warszawy. 17 October 2018. Accessed 1 December 2017 from https://www.polskieradio.pl/39/156/Artykul/957269,Fryderyk-Chopin-Zabierzcie-przynajmniej-serce-me-do-Warszawy [translation by author].

[6] E. Kiewnarska, 109 potraw.Warszawa, 1941, p12. [Translation by author].

[7] An equivalent of the Chamber of Commerce

[8] A shop where desirable Western goods (including jeans and Coca-Cola) could have been obtained for Western currencies

[9] A. Quinn, (2017). Chopin's Heart Pickled in a Jar Offers Clues to His Death. Retrieved 9 December, 2017 from http://www.nytimes.com/2017/11/06/arts/chopin-heart-tuberculosis.html.

[10] Wprost. Polscy naukowcy odkryli przyczynę śmierci Fryderyka Chopina. 1 November 2017. Accessed 9 December 2017, from https://www.wprost.pl/kraj/10084137/polscy-naukowcy-odkryli-przyczyne-smierci-fryderyka-chopina.html

Tourist in my Homeland

by Yin F. Lim

'Cabin crew, please prepare for landing.'

My body tenses up as soon as I hear the captain's announcement and the thud of the landing gear being lowered. I don't much like flying, and enjoy landings even less. Trying to ignore the whine of the wing flaps extending, I peer through the cabin window to focus on the landscape below: neat rows of oil palms, lush green against the occasional swathe of barren land. As we continue our descent, the rays of the late afternoon sun are almost blinding as they catch on the aircraft's wingtip.

Grey tarmac comes into view. I close my eyes and clutch the arms of my seat. The plane judders as soon as the wheels touch the ground and a loud roar fills the aircraft. Pressing myself further into the seat, I tighten my grip on its arms even as the plane propels me forward. My body feels like it's about to be pulled apart by opposing forces. Then the pressure eases as the plane taxies towards its gate.

Back on land. After twelve hours, I can finally walk out of this great, flying hulk that's carried us across continents and oceans. I have no regrets about leaving behind its stale air, its overheated food and outdated entertainment, its crumpled blankets and crushed cups; the detritus of five hundred fellow travellers. But it's not just relief that I feel upon finally arriving at my destination.

'Kepada warganegara Malaysia, selamat pulang ke tanahair.'

Over the PA system, the flight attendant welcomes all returning Malaysians. I can feel a smile forming on my face; I see Nick do the same when I catch his eye over our son Khay's head. We are home.

Leaving the airport terminal, I am hit by a blast of heat and humidity. Pushing my luggage trolley takes twice the effort, making my already-heavy head feel worse. How did we ever live in such a climate, I wonder, tugging my shirt away from my clammy skin as we walk across the parking lot to collect our rental car.

'Air-con please!' Khay insists as we finally settle ourselves in the vehicle. At the turn of a dial, chilled air streams out of the vents, bringing the temperature to a more comfortable level. We pull out of the car park and onto the highway, squinting against the bright sunshine and the shimmery lines on the road in front of us; a mirage created by the heat rising from the bitumen. My jet-lagged brain marvels at how surreal this all feels. Less than 24 hours before, we were driving on another highway

– the M25 – towards London's Heathrow, in a gloomy, drizzly England. Now, as I stare at a large sign that reads 'Kuala Lumpur', it feels as if we never left Malaysia in the first place. Twelve hours and 10,000 km – that's what it takes to get from one world to another. From one home to another.

'So, when will I see Mabel and Kai?' Khay asks from the back seat, impatient to meet up with his cousins. For our 13-year-old son, who left the country when he was 3, our annual visits to Malaysia are fun holidays with extended family. But for Nick and myself every arrival in Kuala Lumpur – or KL, as locals call it – is a homecoming. This is our country of birth, where we had built a life of over forty years before moving to the UK a decade ago. This is home to many milestones, from my first day at school to my first job and first house. This is where Nick and I met, at university, where we graduated and began our careers, where we got married and became parents.

It's a return to the familiar. A return to where we know how things work and who to ask. Where much-loved faces welcome us.

'Have you eaten?'

My mother calls out to us with her customary greeting, a broad smile wrinkling her face as she manoeuvres stiff joints down the front step. Wrapping an arm around Khay's shoulders, she ushers us into her house, our home for the next month.

'Yes,' I reply, wheeling my suitcase into her living room, my bare toes tingling from the cool of the marble floor. From the airport we had driven to the hawker food centre where I ate proper curry *laksa* in true Malaysian style: perched on a rickety stool, head bent over the steaming bowl of noodles, sweat streaming down my face from both the tropical heat and spicy food, savouring every mouthful.

> **I ate proper curry laksa in true Malaysian style: perched on a rickety stool, head bent over the steaming bowl of noodles, sweat streaming down my face**

'Good, you can have some *chendol* then!' Mum laughs as she catches my look of delight at the mention of my favourite dessert. I flop onto a sofa and immediately I'm enveloped by its comforting scent; a musty mix of aged plush, hair cream and memories.

'Careful!' Keay, my youngest brother, tells his 6-year-old daughter, Mabel. She nearly collides into him as she runs to her room, followed by Khay and 9-year-old Kai.

Soon, we are enjoying ice-cold bowls of coconut milk and palm sugar *chendol* as we catch up with everyone's news. My head is whirring along with the ceiling fan above as I try to keep up with the cacophony of 'did-you-know-*ahs*' and 'you-didn't-tell-me-*lahs*,' all intermingled with the children's shouts and laughter.

Suddenly my phone rings, BC's name flashing on the screen. I had sent my friend a text as soon as we landed. I move to a quiet room to answer her call.

'Welcome home! I can't wait to see you both. When can we meet?'

I match the smile I can hear in her voice: 'How about tomorrow morning, breakfast at Raju's?'

We continue chatting as if we had just spoken to each other yesterday, slipping back into the rhythm of our decades-old friendship. BC asks how long we'll be back in town.

'Four weeks,' I say, laughing at her excited gasp as she lists all the new food places we can try together.

—

'So, what do you do for four weeks in KL – won't you get bored? Why don't you come and visit us?'

We're having dinner with my brother-in-law Danny, who's travelled from Singapore to see us. He can't understand how we are able to spend a month in one place. But for Nick and I, it's not just any place, and four weeks is never enough time for everything we need to do.

The first two weeks of our annual trips are akin to reuniting with an old lover – everything's so intense ... none of us wanting to end the hours of non-stop chatter as we make up for our absence in each other's lives

There'll be visits to our former neighbourhood of Sri Damansara to see Elaine, our hairdresser from before Khay was born. Trips to the local supermarket to stock up on prawn paste and Milo malt powder to see us through the winter months in England. Rushing to Raju's after Sunday morning Mass to enjoy crispy *roti canai* flatbread and sweet *teh tarik* under the leafy shade of ancient trees. Morning walks at Bukit Kiara Park before the day gets too hot.

Four weeks a year is hardly any time to reconnect with old friends. The school and university mates with whom I had studied, partied and travelled, whose weddings and children's birthdays I had attended, the same children who are now off to university themselves. The former colleagues with whom I had spent years working late nights on a fledgling newspaper, supporting each other as we cried over setbacks and celebrated successes. And four weeks a year is never long enough with family. With nephews and nieces who've grown taller and bigger since we last saw them, their youthful vigour a sharp contrast to the slower gaits of their grandparents, whose ageing seems more pronounced each year.

The first two weeks of our annual trips are akin to reuniting with an old lover – everything's so intense. We'll meet with friends for early dinners that evolve into late-night suppers, none of us wanting to end the hours of non-stop chatter as we make up for our absence in each other's lives. We'll revisit favourite food stalls and restaurants to satiate months-old cravings, as if it's remotely possible to hoard flavours and tastes to last us until next time. The food has never tasted better, loved ones never seemed more dear, old haunts never more meaningful.

But when you've been apart from your lover, it's easy to ignore the flaws. And this old lover can be very seductive. Before long we find we've slipped back into the cadence of our former lives.

We walk faster, trying to keep up with the city's hustle-bustle. We abandon courteous driving for defensive tactics that help us manoeuvre the manic Malaysian traffic. Muscle memory kicks in and we automatically know which back lanes to take to bypass gridlocked roads. We revert to Malaysian English or Manglish – the mash-up of English, Malay and various Chinese dialects that we grew up speaking.

'Aunty, one plate of *char kway teow ah*. *Tambah* chilli but no *taugeh*.' I order my fried noodles with extra chilli and no bean sprouts at the neighbourhood *kopi tiam* where we're having dinner with Danny. At another food stall, Nick requests Hainanese chicken rice, speaking in Cantonese before switching to Malay as he gives our drinks order to a tall man balancing a glass-laden tray on his palm: '*Bagi teh limau ais satu, Coke satu, Milo ais satu.*'

'It's so easy to become Malaysian again,' Nick says once we are seated at a wobbly table, waiting for our orders to arrive. Yes, it's impossible to resist the draw of all that is comforting and familiar. This busy *kopi tiam* for instance, with its bright fluorescent lighting and hawker stalls offering all kinds of street food, from the smoky *char kway teow* wok-fried over an open fire to the chicken wings sizzling on a charcoal grill.

'Do you think you could live here again?' Danny asks between mouthfuls of his Hokkien fried noodles. I place my chopsticks on my plate and look around at the diners seated nearby. Like us, they've opted to sit outdoors by the roadside where there's a better chance of catching a cool breeze than inside the coffee shop. Amidst snatches of conversation, I can hear pots clanging, vendors shouting, children crying, cars honking, motorcycles roaring – for many years the soundtrack of my life.

Could I live here again?

Malaysia is where I feel complete. It's where I return to retrieve the missing pieces of myself, to rediscover the person I was in the first forty years of my life. I may have left my homeland, but I've come to realise that it's never quite left me – that part of me only truly comes alive when I'm on Malaysian soil. The part that tells me this is where I belong, this store of countless memories. Snippets of teenage chats with my best friend Wendy come to mind whenever I drive around my childhood neighbourhood, past the newsagent where we would swoon over teen idols immortalised in magazine posters. Fragments of nursery rhymes play in my head along with a vision of energetic toddlers, every time I walk by the church hall where I used to take Khay to playgroup.

But could I really live here again?

I take a deep breath and immediately regret it; I've just inhaled a lungful of the noxious fumes emitting from the cars driving past. Coughing hard, I reach for my drink only to find an empty glass. Nick stops a young woman walking past with a tray.

'*Bagi air kosong satu*,' he says in Malay, only to be met with a blank stare. He tries again in Cantonese, the most common Chinese dialect in KL. She remains silent, uncomprehending.

'She's probably from China*lah*,' Danny says, before speaking to the waitress in Mandarin. Recognition registers on her face as she nods and walks off to fetch my water. 'There are so many migrant workers in the coffee shops these days, it's becoming more difficult to order anything.' He's referring to the way we've always relied on instinct – honed through years of living in Malaysia's multicultural, multilingual society – to identify which language to use whenever we speak to someone.

I take a gulp of water and lift my chopsticks to continue eating. From the corner of my eye I spy a sudden movement near an overflowing rubbish bin. A small furry shadow, long tail flickering, scuttles into the open drain. Suddenly, my half-finished plate of *char kway teow* no longer looks so appealing. I quickly turn to Nick and Danny.

'Hey, are we finished yet? Let's go soon.'

—

A silver Perodua MyVi pulls up to the pavement. I quickly check the registration plate against my Grab car-sharing app before I open the door and greet my driver.

'I'm Pang,' the young man responds in Manglish. 'You going to Mont Kiara, right.' I climb into the back seat.

I catch Pang's eyes reflected in the rear-view mirror before he turns away, preparing to re-join the stream of traffic. Instinct tells me he might be more comfortable conversing in Cantonese, so I take a chance and reply in the dialect.

'Do you know the way?'

I can see his shoulders relaxing as he switches languages.

'Yes, I have Waze,' he says, pointing to the popular GPS app on the smartphone clamped to his dashboard. I settle back into the seat as

Instinct tells me he might be more comfortable conversing in Cantonese, so I take a chance and reply in the dialect. 'Do you know the way?'

Pang navigates towards the New Klang Valley Expressway. As he drives, we discuss the state of KL's traffic and what prompted him to become a Grab car driver. Suddenly, he glances at me in the mirror. 'You're not from around here, are you?'

Slightly taken aback by his question, I look out of the window before responding.

'Of course I am. I've lived in KL for most of my life.' I nod firmly, attempting to give weight to my reply.

'Really? But your Cantonese doesn't have a local accent.' He sounds perplexed as he tries to figure me out.

Although I grew up speaking Cantonese, I've never had a good command of the dialect, thanks to years of schooling in the national language of Malay, working in an English-speaking environment and favouring Manglish at home. But this is the first time anyone in Malaysia has ever commented on it.

'It doesn't?' I turn back to Pang. I'm not sure whether to feel affronted or ashamed. 'I live overseas now,' I say, finally.

I catch his grin in the mirror.

'Ahh, that's why *lah*!'

As we discuss life in the UK compared to Malaysia, the inside of the car suddenly grows dim. We're passing through a corridor of limestone hills; high walls loom on both sides of the highway. I spy hazy shapes on the horizon and a feeling of anticipation runs through me. Any moment now, the corridor will open out to present my favourite view of the city's skyline: a series of glimmering skyscrapers, the tapering needle of the KL Tower at one end and the twin rockets of the Petronas Towers at the other.

I can barely make out the gleaming tip of the KL Tower beyond the roof of one dull block, like a crumb left behind on the greedy lip of this monster of development

We leave the hills, but all I can see ahead of me is a cluster of condominium buildings, uniform in their oblong shapes and beige facades. I can barely make out the gleaming tip of the KL Tower beyond the roof of one dull block, like a crumb left behind on the greedy lip of this monster of development.

'Hey, what happened? What are all those condos?' I turn to Pang, trying to control my dismay.

'That's Mont Kiara, where we're going.'

'There never used to be so many blocks.' I protest.

'*Waah*, you haven't been here for a long time *ah*,' Pang shakes his head, and we leave the highway.

Half an hour later, I am inside one of those same condominium blocks, listening to my friends from university discuss the corruption scandal that has implicated Prime Minister Najib Tun Razak and triggered a leadership crisis.

'More than two billion ringgit and he's still in office. Can you believe it? In other countries, they would have made him resign!' Mei is almost shouting as she sets down a plate on the table in front of me. The slice of cheesecake quivers from the force of her anger.

Najib has been accused of channelling two billion ringgit from 1MDB, a company connected to the government, to his personal accounts. Investigative reporting by the media has uncovered a network of international fund transfers, leading to bank accounts being frozen and the US Justice Department initiating legal action to seize assets allegedly purchased with the misappropriated funds.

'Look, look, doesn't this make you sick!' Mei's husband Lam scowls as he shoves his smartphone in front of me. It's playing a video of Najib telling journalists that his government is serious about good governance, that they will fully cooperate with the investigations. 'Talk about a hypocrite!" Lam flings his arms in the air.

'What's happening to our country?' Mei presses her fingers against her temples as if to soothe an ache that won't go away.

I stay silent, unsure how to contribute. I share my friends' alarm about my homeland. I'm saddened that there's not much they can do until the next general elections are called – not for another two years. But I can't help feeling like a spectator as I listen to them, unable to match their level of anger and despair. More than anything, their emotional state reminds me how I felt after the EU referendum. I shift in my chair and stare at the slice of cheesecake.

'You guys are so lucky you no longer live here,' Lam remarks, not without a hint of envy. I silently agree with him and the relief I feel is tempered by guilt, for having 'run away' from our country and its problems, even though we left long before the 1MDB scandal broke.

'Yeah but don't forget, we've got Brexit,' I reply at last.

The conversation trails off. The three of us sit in silence, eating our cake.

Over dinner that night, I try to explain my sense of disquiet to Nick while the kids huddle over a tablet. We are having dinner at a seafood restaurant called Fish & Co, as Khay has been clamouring for fish and chips.

'Yeah, I know what you mean,' Nick replies as he tells me about his meeting with former colleagues earlier that day. 'After a while, I felt we were running out of things to say to one other. Every year I come back we have less and less in common. I barely know what and who they talk about.' My husband muses as he flicks his thumb against the restaurant menu. 'They've moved on – but I guess I've changed too.'

I'm about to reply when a howl interrupts us.

'What's this? It's not even real fish and chips!'

The waiter has placed a large plate in front of Khay. On it is a flat square coated in orange breadcrumbs next to a mound of crispy fries and a pile of peas. It looks nothing like the fish and chips from our local chippy back in England.

'But these ARE chips!' Kai says as he pops one in his mouth.

'Hey! You didn't ask if you could have one!' Khay stands up to glare at Kai as Mabel looks on, mouth

On [the plate] is a flat square coated in orange breadcrumbs next to a mound of crispy fries and a pile of peas. It looks nothing like the fish and chips from our local chippy back in England

open. 'And they're not chips, they're skinny fries!' I can feel eyes upon us.

'Sit down and eat your food,' I glare at my son. Khay obeys, sulking, but refuses to touch his meal. A young waitress walks over, a friendly smile on her face.

'*Dik, kenapa tak makan? Ikan ni sedap!*' Speaking in Malay, she asks Khay why he isn't eating the delicious fish. He looks at her blankly.

'Ma, what's she saying?' Khay turns towards me and so does the waitress, her eyes wide.

'*Eh, dia cakap macam orang puteh. Dia tak faham ke?*' She's startled by my son's British accent and asks if he understands.

I shake my head and explain that Khay has never learnt Malay: '*Dia tak belajar Bahasa Malaysia. Kami tinggal diluar negeri.*'

This is the second time today I've had to explain that we no longer live in Malaysia. I'm beginning to feel more and more like a tourist in my homeland.

———

The afternoon downpour has subsided. The wiper blades have left a watery sheen on the windscreen, transforming the tail lights ahead of us into a blur of red and orange. We're in the middle of the city, inching forwards at what feels like half a mile per hour. Drivers around us, never patient even on a normal day, vent their frustration through their car horns.

I look at the clock on the dashboard and let out a loud groan.

'At this rate, we'll be lucky if we arrive in time for dessert.'

Nick frowns at the traffic-choked road in front of us. 'It's worse than the M25 on a bad day.'

I turn my head to peer out the window. Under the hazy glow of street lights, I can see rivulets of muddy water running down the side of the road by the grassy verge.

'Are we there yet?' Khay's voice, thick with sleep, drifts towards us from the back seat. Bored with the delay, he dozed off half an hour ago.

'Nearly there, Khay. Look.'

I point to my left, where I can see the curved tower block that is the Shangri-La Hotel. Its lit windows, glowing against the dusky sky, beckon us. It's close enough for us to reach in five minutes of fast walking, but we can't just abandon the car in the middle of the road. We were meant to arrive thirty minutes ago for dinner with Nick's family. We thought we'd given ourselves ample time to get to the city centre, even taking into account how KL comes to a standstill after a monsoon deluge. But instead of following Waze, we had relied on our increasingly obsolete knowledge of local roads and had to backtrack. I glare at my husband who is oblivious to my annoyance.

Pulling my cardigan around me as a shield against the air-conditioning's chill, I turn towards the back seat.

'I know, you wish you were in Por-Por's house with Mabel and Kai instead, right?'

Khay shoots me a look I can't quite decipher.

'Actually, no. It's nice to have some peace and quiet.'

I raise my eyebrows as Nick throws me a bemused glance. The three cousins have been inseparable since we arrived in KL. The first thing Khay asks when he wakes up is when he'll see them next.

'No? You're getting tired of them already?' Nick asks.

Khay huffs before replying.

'They make so much noise. Mabel and Kai are always fighting, and I have to be the peacemaker.' He's quiet for a second, before adding: 'I wish I was home. I miss my room. I miss England.'

I face forwards again toward the sea of orange and red; it doesn't look like we've moved at all. Khay's mention of England is an invocation. Suddenly I too wish I were in my own home, sleeping in my own bed, baking in my own kitchen. I want to hear birdsong early in the morning and stillness late at night, instead of constant background noise from the TV or traffic. I want to smell the heady lavender in my garden instead of rank, clogged drains by the roadside. I miss food shopping at our local Sainsbury's, and walking or cycling to the city centre. If we were in Norwich, we wouldn't be stuck in traffic like this. We would have been on time.

A few days later I'm in the suburb of Bangsar, trudging up a gently inclined road to reach the shopping mall. As I navigate my way over loose gravel, dodging puddles of stagnant water, I can

Just a few more days, I tell myself. Just a few more days and I'll be back where I don't break out in a sweat at the slightest exhalation

feel the heat emanating from my body, my face flushed from the exertion and humidity. Just a few more days, I tell myself. Just a few more days and I'll be back where I don't break out in a sweat at the slightest exhalation.

A day before we're due to leave, Nick and I are in my mother's living room with my brother Seng, who is telling us about a meeting at his son's school.

'So I told the teacher he won't be coming to school on Monday, but then she was like, you know...' Seng opens his palms in an upward gesture as he looks at me expectantly.

'No, I don't know!' I snap at him; I immediately feel terrible. My brother can't help it if I now find exasperating what a few weeks ago had seemed endearingly familiar – the way most Malaysians never complete a sentence because we assume our listener understands what we mean. I'm about to apologise when we hear a screech upstairs.

'Mabel!'

Three sets of footsteps thunder down the stairs. Khay runs to us, followed by his cousins.

'Ma, Mabel messed up our game!'

'Yeah, she took Khay's iPad!' Kai chips in.

'No, I didn't!' My niece's face crumples as she starts to wail.

'You know, it really is time to go home,' Nick says.

———

'Returning?' The Border Agency officer at London Heathrow greets us as he scans our residence permits.

'Yes,' I say. The word runs through my head: returning. That means coming back to something. I'm returning to my home in the UK. Another homecoming.

'Welcome back,' the officer smiles as he waves us through.

As we exit the airport terminal, a breeze on my face lifts my jet-lagged daze. It's invigorating after a month of smothering heat and freezing air-conditioning. Approaching a zebra crossing, I wait for cars to pass before stepping onto the road.

'What are you doing? You can go. We're back in England now,' Nick nudges me with his elbow before pushing his luggage trolley in front of the car that's stopped for us.

'So, can we get some fish and chips?' Khay bounces on the pavement as we load luggage into our car. As he climbs into the back seat, he rattles off a list of what he plans to do the moment he arrives home.

Later, on the M11, I'm reminded of how civilised British drivers are. There's no incessant honking, no motorists overtaking one another, no daredevil motorcyclists weaving between vehicles. I look out my window at the English countryside, so gentle and soothing. The concrete jungle that is KL, the constant bustle that is Asia, feels very distant.

Groping in my cardigan pocket for some tissue, I find a small piece of paper instead. It's a ticket stub for the circus performance we attended a week ago. I stare down at the creased face of a clown and can hear the children laughing. I can see my mother's beaming face, her eyes soft and her lower lip caught between her teeth as she reaches out to ruffle my son's hair.

I shove the ticket back into my pocket and turn quickly towards Nick, trying to control the wobble in my voice.

'Look at how green everything is. It must have rained a lot this summer.' **H**

The Royal Society *of* Literature

RSL Autumn events include:

Friday 13 September
7pm, National Portrait Gallery
Imitation of Life
Marking the major retrospective of Cindy Sherman; Adjoa Andoh, Esther Freud, Bonnie Greer and Sophie Mackintosh discuss performance in writing, image and on stage.

Monday 23 September
7pm, British Library
***Banned Books Week:
Walled In***
David Hare and Ben Okri consider walls in literature and in our lives, thirty years after the Berlin Wall was pulled down.

Tuesday 12 November
7pm, British Library
Black in the Union Jack?
Jeffrey Boakye, Paul Gilroy and Derek Owusu take a panoramic look at global Black history and Black British experience, past and present.

Friday 29 November
7pm, King's College London
Writing lives
Lara Feigel, Delia Jarrett-Macauley, Anthony Joseph and Hermione Lee explore the self-reflective aspect of writing experimental auto-fiction, memoir and biography.

RSL Giles St Aubyn Awards for Non-Fiction now open for submissions

The RSL is currently accepting submissions for the third year of the RSL Giles St Aubyn Awards for Non-Fiction. **Two awards** – one of **£10,000**, one of **£5,000** – are offered to support writers to complete their first commissioned works of non-fiction. They present an extraordinary opportunity to realise the full potential of the book to come.

More information
rsliterature.org

There are no Polar Bears where I live

by Martin Eberlen

This is not a story. A crisis is engulfing the world we live in, felt by communities across the globe. Whilst our days, especially here, where I live in London, do not begin quite so dramatically fires continue to burn, ferociously, across the land that we once so delicately tended. With our world in the midst of environmental catastrophe, I often wonder what it might take for people to become more attuned to the scale of such devastation.

For many urban communities a direct relationship with nature has almost vanished; for others it has become severely disjointed. Pockets of land that appear wild and untouched have become battlegrounds that, without sufficient protection, are rapidly captured, crushing vital ecosystems barely visible to the naked eye. Instead of allowing these spaces to flourish naturally, we weave and craft a designed vision of outdoor spaces, cramming

them in as an afterthought between high-rise, unaffordable apartment blocks. Under the wrath of consumerism, forgotten corners of residential streets have gradually built up a collection of unwanted impulse buys, fast-food wrappers, and unsightly furniture. Weeds engulf this mess, attempting to force a process of decomposition over manufactured materials and, failing to do so, end up preserving these items for future generations.

Glance left, then right. It is safe. There are no polar bears where I live. They're hungry though. I know this because I've seen the pictures on the news. It was bin day today. My neighbour's trash has been dragged across the street, torn open, and abandoned: foxes. They're OK. They've got food.

Light, floating rain. Drizzle.

Been out for one minute. Soaked. Thinking about turning back; I turn back. I stop. Turn around again. Then again; and again. I just walked in a circle, on the spot. Twice. Nutter. A discarded can in the bush catches my eye. That's why I'm walking today. Because I don't understand. I carry on.

Marvels Lane. Sounds like a place where superheroes live. It's not. Drizzle. Drizzle. Drizzle. The outskirts of South East London. Hardly a tourist destination. Saying that, I'm the one who bought a book to guide me along this 'hidden corridor of green space.'

There's a sign for a missing dog.

I want to see where the people live. Where the rhythm of life is just one beat slower than the city six miles north. Drizzle. Drizzle is along for the ride.

A few miles in, I haven't seen another person. I've seen ten posters for missing dogs though. Perhaps the dogs aren't missing. Perhaps it's like that film, *Isle of Dogs*, but instead of humans sending them away they're just leaving of their own accord. Because they know what's coming.

It's weird, I don't see anyone else. Nobody going in the opposite direction. There's signs of human life: the warm orange glow from windows as I pass. People around, but they're not walking with me. They're inside. Too right. It's cold out here. There's nothing but rain and concrete and broken dreams – sorry, broken chairs. Why is there a couch in a bush? Legs are a little tired actually. I could do with a sit down. But not there. I'd get a wet arse.

Gardens. Plastic bins. Plastic bags full of plastic things. Prams and scooters, children's swings. All broken.

The drizzle stops.

A fox. I try and get its attention. 'Here boy. Heyyyyy hey heyyyy hey hey hey. Stop!' I'm a mad man again. The fox doesn't understand. Why am I telling it to stop? Am I expecting it to turn and say 'Yeah? What's up? I'm just off to the bins, you want anything?'

It stops. Looks at me. Carries on.

Trees. I'm surrounded. I'm impressed. Ignore the dog shit on the floor.

Sparrow. Squirrel. Blue tit. Robin. Wren. Blackbird. Squirrel. Wood pigeon. Squirrel. Wood pecker. Squirrel. Green Finch. Squirrel. Lots of squirrels.

Shit. I'm hungry. Café. Inside.

What have you got that's gluten free?

Errr...nothing.

What about the soup?

It's got chickpeas in it.

Chickpeas don't have gluten in them, you idiot, I want to say; but don't.

I nod politely. Never mind.

I've got a banana in my bag. Peel it. Eat it. Chuck the skin in a bush...I'm the problem.

Ohhhhh. Nice houses here. Even the alleyways are clean.

Neat park. A dog chases a ball. There's a bee. A bee? In January? Forget the bee. It's probably fine. This park is... Plastic bag caught in a branch.

Drizzle? Nope. Rain.

Palm trees. Shivering. I want to wrap them in electric blankets.

Voices. At last. I'm not alone. Kids though. Ugh.
She's drinking Coke from a can. He's throwing
stones at a swan. He runs out of stones.

'Throw this,' she says, gesturing with her can.

He doesn't.

She does.

They turn around and see me.

'Did you just throw that can in the river?'

He frowns, aggressively.

Something inside me tells me to walk away.

She says 'It slipped out my hand.'

I lower my head; feel the gentle trickle of drizzle
landing on the back of my neck. I close my eyes. ▣

The photographs for this work were produced in the scope of
PARALLEL European Photo Based Platform.

Yeoyu —— new voices Korea

Han Kang
Bae Suah
Han Yujoo
Kim Soom
Kang Hwagil
Jeon Sungtae
Cheon Heerahn
Hwang Jungeun

KANG HWAGIL

강화길

DEMONS

TRANSLATED BY MATTHO WANDERSLOES

손

KON
G'S
GAR
DEN

HWANG JUNGEUN

양의
미래

전승희

황정은

TRANSLATED BY JEON SEUNG-HEE

Parasites
and

Autoclaves

by Kate Romain

I feel his arm against my back, stretching the length of my chair; his fingertips, light, at first, beneath my shoulder blade, and then heavier, pressing into my skin. They catch, for a moment, on the strap of my bra. And he keeps looking at me. I can tell from the angle of his face, even as I try my best to ignore it, to keep looking straight ahead. I can *feel* him looking at me, the same as I can feel his arm around me, his lingering fingers like a constant, unexpected tap on the shoulder, intended to remind me that somebody is there.

The walls of the bar are painted black and covered in chalky scribblings. Earlier in the evening, during dinner at a nearby restaurant, he had told me about this; said we would have to think of something to add, something witty. Or failing that, he joked, we could just write our names in the centre of a heart.

The bar itself feels as crowded as the walls, and we were lucky to find this table at all. A man and a woman had seen us, still wrapped in our coats, cocktails in our hands, and gestured to the two empty seats at their long wooden table. From the way they lean in close to one another as they talk; from her warm, attentive smile and his earnest reciprocation; more simply, from their being together at this bar, just the two of them, on a Friday night, I imagine they are probably on a date too.

The band in front of us plays on, their knees bending, feet tapping, their torsos, from the waist up, bending back and forth, to the beat of their music. Their dancing isn't fluid, or graceful, but there is nothing self-conscious or mechanical about their performance. That they have performed cover after cover; that their hair is thinning and their round stomachs protrude above the buckles of their belts; that their shirts strain to reveal small patches of pale skin; that they likely list their professions as accountants, web-designers, retail managers; where official documentation is concerned, doesn't seem to matter. Nor does it matter that they are playing to an anonymous crowd in an anonymous basement bar in a small town in the middle of the Midwest.

A group of friends, several girls and a few boys who I think must have fake IDs appear at the edge of the bar. They stand in front of the band and glance around the room, before sitting at a large round table that has recently become vacant. One of the girls sits on the lap of another, leans in close to talk to her friends, and then calls out to someone sitting at the opposite side of the table. They all look completely at ease with one another, and with themselves. I think it is admirable that they have achieved this at such a young age, wish that I had been the same way. Wonder, even if I have achieved it now. But when I use my imagination to strip them of their makeup and matchingly mismatched outfits and down to their essences, to their fresh faces and un-styled hair, I would not necessarily put them together, as friends. *Isn't that funny*, I think, *how some faces belong together, and others don't? And how in this instance, the incompatibility of their faces doesn't seem to matter?*

This, the second half of a second date, a week and a half after a fairly standard first date: a slightly drunken, slightly hazy, fairly enjoyable evening at a dive bar

And then those fingers on my back again, belonging to Harvey, my date for the evening; this, the second half of a second date, a week and a half after a fairly standard first date: a slightly drunken, slightly hazy, fairly enjoyable evening at a dive bar followed by a comedy club. It had been an evening peppered with, but not ruined by, a few vaguely concerning, perhaps best overlooked, indiscretions of his: an irritating turn of phrase here; a clumsy political comment there; a few unwarranted, lingering looks. But we had laughed in the right places during each other's stories, and ultimately, it had been fun.

The couple beside us bend their heads low and close together over the table, smiling at something on the woman's phone. He whispers something in her ear and she laughs loudly and earnestly. I look at Harvey, try to discern whether I find him attractive, but I can't. In some lights, he's quite good-looking, but being good-looking and being attractive aren't the same thing, and I've noticed I don't like the way he walks. The couple sitting beside us begin to kiss. I can see in my peripherals Harvey's elbow sticking out from the back of my chair at a peculiar angle, and he twists his body to accommodate it, reaching further across my shoulders, trapping my hair between his forearm and my own back as he does so. I try to turn my head, and feel a dull tug at the bottom of my scalp. Though I try to ignore it, I feel restricted; I couldn't move to the beat of the music if I wanted to. I lean forwards to free myself. He jerks his arm backwards and away from me, as if I had burnt him. He looks at me, lost, and then embarrassed, and then, is that annoyance? It passes so quickly, the bar is so dark, that I can't tell. I smile an involuntary apology.

'There's something about you,' he says, his voice quiet and lost beneath the music, as if he is confessing something intimate and gentle and fleeting that I must make the effort to capture, 'that makes me feel so awkward.'

I'm shocked. This was not my intention. I feel a surge of guilt for accepting this second date when I had the hunch – no, I knew, the way one always knows these things, if they take the time to really listen to themselves – that whereas he wanted a physical relationship with me, I probably would not be wanting one with him, despite earlier this evening taking the precaution of shaving my legs. I feel like a trickster. I feel socially inept. Does he feel awkward in my presence because I am so worldly, fascinating, cool, and anyone would feel ill at ease around such a presence; or because I am the exact opposite; because I am confusing, slippery, muddled?

'I'm sorry,' I say.

'Don't be,' he says.

A lone man with an angular jaw and thin grey hair, a red button-down shirt cinched at the waist with a black leather belt fastened to a pair of blue jeans, slides across the dance floor, pointing rhythmically around the room; a dance inspired in equal parts by Michael Jackson's Moonwalk and John Travolta in *Saturday Night Fever*. He looks into my eyes and beckons me, searching for a dance partner and hoping that I might be it. I smile and shake my head.

'You should dance with him,' Harvey teases.

'I can't dance,' I say.

The red-shirted man beckons the woman beside me. Her reaction is the same as mine. He beckons one of the girls at the round table, and suddenly she is up, dancing with him, holding his hands and twirling, her hips swaying back and forth beneath a floating blue skirt; her hair, some of which she has fastened in a loose bun, swings about her face. He does not hold her waist, though I imagine he would like to, but falls into step with her, no longer sliding but leaping and shaking, matching her high energy. And for her, I think, as she grins and dances, there is nothing in this but fun. I think she looks beautiful.

'Oh man,' Harvey says. 'I bet he's been waiting his whole life for this!'

'Most definitely,' I say. I smile from behind my glass, reach for my phone from beneath the table to record a snippet of the unlikely dance partners to upload to my Instagram story, and notice I'm not the only person in the bar doing so.

When the song is over the pair hug, his arms square around her shoulders. The bar cheers and

> **I smile from behind my glass, reach for my phone from beneath the table to record a snippet of the unlikely dance partners to upload to my Instagram story,**

the girl beams, her hands clasped, her face pink and laughing, graciously accepting her applause. The old man bows theatrically.

'Amazing,' I say. Harvey has removed his arm from around me to clap, and now, for the time being, is contained in his own chair. I finish the remainder of my drink. His glass is already empty. He gestures vaguely at the table.

'Another drink?' he asks.

I do not have to consider my response, and this, I think, might be my failing.

'OK,' I say. 'I'll just get a Jameson's this time, please.'

'It's your round, isn't it?' he says.

'It's my round?' I raise my eyebrows slightly, remembering the several tabs I had picked up last week, the first time we went out; the bowl I fries we had split that I had paid for; his asking me for a cigarette, my suggesting we go and buy some, and his subsequent failure to buy a pack of his own; the way he had immediately said: 'Oh! They didn't split the check. Lets just throw down two cards,' after tonight's dinner.

'I think so,' he says.

I move to pull my wallet from my purse. I wonder: is this what it means to be a modern woman?

'What do you want?' I ask.

'Same as you?'

'OK.'

I go to the bar to order the drinks. When I return, he is fiddling with a piece of chalk, making small white marks on the wooden table top and then wiping it clean with the side of his hand.

'Chalk?' I say.

'Yes. I think I saw some space on the other side, over there, near the bar. We still need to think of something clever to write. No pressure.'

I look towards the band and he, once again, looks at me, and I joke lamely with myself that all of us together must make up a sort of dissatisfied trio, always gazing, yet never having our gazes met

'No pressure,' I repeat. 'OK.'

I look towards the band and he, once again, looks at me, and I joke lamely with myself that all of us together must make up a sort of dissatisfied trio, always gazing, yet never having our gazes met. And now he is looking at my hands. I become aware of the way they are placed in my lap, the fingers of the right clamped loosely around the palm of the left. Suddenly this looks, and feels, unnatural. Do my hands look like they want to be held? I slide them further down my lap, beneath the table, out of view.

Something to say: 'Do you reckon these guys are the headliners? Or is Jimi Hendrix coming on after this?'

'What?'

He leans in close to me, pinching my sleeve and rubbing it beneath his fingers, as if he is evaluating the thread count. His ear is close to my mouth and I lean towards him, so that he can hear me over the band. He in turn leans towards me, and I feel his arm on the back of my chair pressing into me a little more firmly as his weight adjusts and I am relieved to think that this physical contact might now be for the purposes of practicality, as opposed to romance.

'I said, are these guys the headliners? Or the warm up for Jimi Hendrix?'

'Oh,' he says, 'definitely a warm up act. Hendrix will be on in five!'

'Good,' I say, 'I'm looking forward to it.'

I look at him sideways, as quickly as I can, mainly out of curiosity. I am afraid that if we make eye contact he will try to kiss me. He is chewing his lower lip and the action is causing his face to contort, and now that his face is no longer symmetrical I conclude it is symmetry he has to thank for his good looks, that they are nothing more than an illusion caused by fortunate proportions.

Suddenly, he turns towards me and holds my left hand, picking it up from my lap and wrapping his fingers around my palm. My hand is completely unsure of what to do with itself, if not performing the most natural response of curling the fingertips back around his own hand, which I absolutely don't want to do, because if I hold his hand he will probably think I also want to kiss him, and I don't. I would just as soon kiss the date of the woman sitting next to me; I am sure I could have had a fairly enjoyable conversation, a fairly enjoyable evening – maybe even as fairly enjoyable, fairly decent, as the first half of this one – with him, had I swiped right for his profile. I hold my hand erect. And there we stay, for a moment, both looking down into my lap with surprise and horror.

He lets go, exhales quickly and heavily, as if lost for words. He moves his head as if to shake it but doesn't follow through.

I want to be kind to him, to relieve his embarrassment; or maybe doing so would be an act of kindness towards myself, because I feel this tension acutely.

I smile and say, 'What?'

I intend to say it softly, to smile kindly, and maybe I succeed.

'You've just made me feel so self-conscious,' he says, sounding brooding, confessional.

What? I think. I feel, once again, like a ridiculous little girl – it is a hand, after all, just an insignificant, harmless hand, my holding of which may or may not lead to an equally insignificant, harmless kiss – except now I felt like a ridiculous little girl who, though well aware of just having been backed into a corner, lacks the means and wherewithal to fight her way out. If touching is so insignificant, I think, then why insist on it?

'I am sorry,' I say, and though I make no attempt to hide my anger and exasperation, I do not allow myself to be carried by it, to say the things I really want to, because I don't know if they'd be justified; how would a ridiculous little girl know whether she is behaving correctly, when she so clearly is oblivious to the effects of her actions on other people? I don't think I ever intended to make him feel awkward.

Why do you want to hold my hand? Why do you keep looking at me? Why are you so determined to look deeply into eyes that are ... determined to avert yours? Why can't you buy your own damn cigarettes?

'Please,' he says, and maybe I'm imagining it, or maybe his tone matches my own, 'don't apologise.'

The small dance floor is beginning to fill. I look for the girl, see her standing, leaning over her table between two of her friends, resting on her elbows, her face cupped in her hands. I see the red-shirted man on the other side of the bar, leaning up against the wall, looking at his phone. The girl stands up from her table and walks across the dancefloor, just a few yards from the man, but he doesn't look up at her, seems completely unaware of her presence. They had their moment, I think, and now their moment has passed. And he respects that.

I tell Harvey I am going to the bathroom and navigate my way through the crowd. I wait for a free cubicle, stare at my feet as I scuff them against the floor. *Why do you want to hold my hand? Why do you keep looking at me? Why are you so determined to look deeply into eyes that are equally as determined to avert yours? Why can't you buy your own damn cigarettes?* I say all this to myself now because I didn't say it to him back then. Not because I am a good person, but because I am a person who lacks conviction. I hang my head lower.

I look up as a woman exits a cubicle, and we exchange smiles. I gather a wad of toilet roll in my fist as I wee, pick at a crumpled square that sticks out from the edge. I sit on the toilet for a minute longer than is necessary, check my Instagram story to see how many people have viewed it. I have no plan, no exit strategy. I haven't tried to make one; I'm unsure if I need one.

I sit on the toilet for a minute longer than is necessary, check my Instagram story to see how many people have viewed it. I have no plan, no exit strategy. I haven't tried to make one; I'm unsure if I need one

I see, upon returning to the table, that he has scrawled an illegible sentence across its top with the chalk. 'What does that say?' I ask, and think, it is impossible to permanently cast a person in the role of the enemy if they are right there in front of you; people are too curious, too lonely, for that.

'It says *my hearts a…*' he trails off and says something that sounds like rocket ship.

'Your heart's a what?'

'An autoclave.'

'What's an autoclave?'

'It's like,' he says, 'it's like this big container they use for high pressure experiments. So it contains, like, all these super high pressure gasses… I know,' he says, 'it's weird.'

I am unaware of how my features have arranged themselves, but they must have betrayed my distaste. I make a half-hearted attempt to readjust them to a more neutral expression.

'You have to write something now,' he says, and holds the chalk in front of me.

'I can't think of anything,' I say, and I really can't. Nothing that I would want to write.

'Come on,' he says, 'you must be able to think of something.'

'I can't!' I say, but I take the chalk from between his fingers.

'Anything!'

I tap the chalk against the table. Of course, there are lots of things I could write, but this can't just be any lyric; this is a request for me lay at least some of my cards on the table; to openly caption this tense situation, made tenser still by his declaration, staring up at me from the table, increasingly legible since being read and explained to me, that his heart is explosive, volatile, dangerous. Not only does he want me to hold his hand, to snuggle into him, he wants me to tell him exactly how I feel about this, about him, about the us that didn't exist two hours ago but now seems to him to be the most important thing; the same us, in any case, I was sure was completely extinguished approximately six minutes ago, when I refuted his ham-fisted and coercive attempts at intimacy. And he wants me to do this in the form of a song lyric, and he wants me to do it now. The chalk is poised above the table.

He says again: 'anything!'

I begin to scrawl. *He wants a song lyric? Fine! He can have one!*

'*Show me someone who's a....* Show me someone who's a what?' he says, reading from the table as I write.

'It's kind of a long lyric,' I say, and it is. By the time I reach the word parasite, I truly regret choosing it, but it's far too late. Why didn't I write something else? Why did I write anything at all?

The lyric is finished, and it seems to me as though it covers the whole of the table.

'Show me someone who's not a... something about... *parasites*? And prayers?' He says.

'It doesn't matter,' I say, embarrassed.

He looks at me as if I am crazy. 'Who sang about *that*?' he says, and scathingly adds: 'Jon Bon Jovi?'

'Bob Dylan,' I say.

'Really?' he says, looking annoyed and disbelieving. 'In which song?'

I no longer regret anything.

'I don't know,' I say, although I do, but I don't want to look like a know-it-all. 'But it was definitely Bob Dylan. He *definitely* sang about parasites and prayers.' With the side of my hand I smear the words, all of them, across the table whilst he looks on. We watch the band in silence for a while longer. I gulp the remainder of my Jameson's and place the empty glass down firmly on the table. There is another bar, one with a live pianist and an extensive whisky menu, that I would like to have gone to next, had this date gone better. I wonder how long, in how-many-drinks-time, it would take me to rectify this situation, so that we could go. At least three, probably, if it could be rectified at all. And that's no good; I'd be falling-down-drunk by then. I prepare to make my excuses and leave.

He turns to me.

'Kate?' he says.

'Yes?' I say.

'Can I kiss you?'

Another song begins. Nearly everyone is on the dance floor, and I can catch only glimpses of the band through the lively crowd.

> **I am both relieved and horrified that he has asked; relieved that he has given me the option to say no and horrified that I now have to respond at all**

'Umm,' I say. I am both relieved and horrified that he has asked; relieved that he has given me the option to say no and horrified that I now have to respond at all. I remember saying once, to a group of people at a party: *there is nothing that irritates me more than when a man asks if he can kiss me.* 'Um, honestly…' I say, 'To be honest, *I* feel a little awkward that… that you said I made you feel awkward.'

Harvey looks back at me, eyes narrowed. Then they widen, and he looks down at the table. He nods. 'Fair enough,' he says.

The girl is dancing again, the red-shirted man once again dancing with her, but now he is draped around her, and several of her friends push between them, trying to peel him away. I look back at Harvey. He looks sheepish and lost. I realise it is time to leave.

'Look,' I say. 'Do you want a cigarette?'

'Desperately,' he says. 'Thanks.' He smiles at me, and I smile back.

I gather my things, make it clear we will not be coming back down. He does the same.

Outside in the cold air, I hand him a cigarette, light my own, and pass him my lighter. We smoke together in silence for a minute. He looks down at his feet.

I can't avoid the silence any longer. He fills it with his face, as I knew he would, and I still don't want to kiss him, but now, I don't not want to either. I am tired of resisting

'It's cold,' I say.

'It is.'

I realise there is nothing left to say about that.

'I just feel a little…' I begin. 'It's just, if it doesn't feel natural, you shouldn't try to force it, I think.'

'Yeah,' he says.

'Like,' I say, 'if it doesn't feel like it's flowing, then…'

'You're right. I'm just new to this.'

I nod: *Yes, you are.* 'Well,' I say, 'I guess it's not easy.'

There is another silence. 'I think, um, honesty is a good thing.' I could say more, but my previous statement felt too much like a prelude to nervous gabbling, and I don't want to do that to myself. There is nothing else for it: I can't avoid the silence any longer. He fills it with his face, as I knew he would, and I still don't want to kiss him, but now, I don't not want to either. I am tired of resisting.

His lips meet mine and move up and down over my mouth, and my mouth does the same in response. It is not awful, it is not spectacular, but a relief; finally, the awkwardness has subsided. The kiss lasts as long as it needs to. My right hand stays in my pocket, my cigarette dangles from the left, held off to one side, and afterwards I duck my lips away from his and towards it to inhale. I notice a group of girls, a little way down the street, who must have walked past us as we were kissing. We must have made for a romantic silhouette, I think, kissing in the dark, standing in the melted snow, beneath the bare branches of a tree hung with fairy-lights.

'See,' I say, 'much better.' And that was true. He grins at me.

'Shall we go?' I say.

Walking down the street towards my house the conversation is much as it was before, over dinner; we talk about the weather, how cold it is here compared to the places we are from; agree that though there is still much of winter left to be endured, we are both looking forward to spring. He makes a point I don't agree with, using a turn of phrase that irks me, but not so much that I address it.

'Well,' I say, once we have reached the end of my street, 'I need to go this way.' He smiles, leans in, and kisses me again. I reciprocate, and then pull away. 'Can I come up,' he says, 'to your house? For a minute?'

'Um, I think I should go... You know, just me,' I say.

'OK,' he says.

'Bye,' I say.

'Bye.'

I leave him and walk down the street towards my house, turn and look over my shoulder to see if he is following me, or, more likely, if he is still standing there, watching me; if he will see which house is mine. He is looking at me, grinning, shaking his head slightly.

I lock the door behind me, remove my coat, pour myself a pint of water and gulp it down. I pour myself another and put it on my bedside table. I open Spotify on my phone, select a jazz playlist at random. Alone, in my bathroom, I leap and slide across the tiles and throw my hands above my head, swaying to the beat of the music. Beneath my dress, I swing my hips, watch my reflection in the bathroom mirror to see if I am dancing as well as the blue-skirted girl. I'm not, of course – I was being honest when I told Harvey I couldn't dance – but I carry on anyway; think that, though I will never have the skill she does, if I keep practicing, keep working on it, keep pushing myself, then, one day, my dancing will be as unselfconscious, as free, as hers. **H**

You thought you knew the whole story...

Come and celebrate with us at Untitled writers' events - a new platform for underrepresented writers to share their work in front of an audience. There are no limitations to what might be shared and we know there'll be something for everyone.

To find out more about Untitled, let us know if you want to share your work in the future and to find news about our next event in October visit **untitledwriting.co.uk**

🐦 writinguntitled   📷 untitled_writing

Rahmania

by Sureshkumar P. Sekar

It is a song like no other; the delicate sound of its music seems to ooze through many infinitesimal yet distinctly perceptible pores of silence. The play and the pause, the loud and the quiet, the heard and the unheard, the movement and the stillness, the sound and the silence – they meet, they mate and then part ways, only to meet again through the course of the song. It is a duet, of two separated lovers each singing the pain of their existence without the other. The song's melody is romantic, the mood melancholic, and the rhythm languorous.

It has been over twenty-four hours since the song was released on iTunes, and as a self-proclaimed Rahmaniac – an ardent fan of the music of A.R. Rahman, the composer of this song – I should have already heard it at least twenty-five times. But I have not.

The release of a new Rahman song is a festival day for Rahmaniacs, and there are rituals one must follow on this auspicious day. Irrespective of where we are or what we do, the single lingering thought in our minds is the new music. We can't wait to stop doing whatever we are doing and run to a quiet space to listen. Passively listening to a new Rahman song is forbidden; it is almost a sin. So I don't play the new song as background music at work, nor do I let it play on a loop while doing chores at home; these bad habits would monotonise the song, make me numb to its melody and mood before I have had the opportunity to dwell in its depths and enjoy its finer pleasures. When I listen to a new Rahman song, I do that and only that. Call it what you may, adulation or meditation, that's how I like it.

This is a special relationship, the one between Rahman and his ardent followers. He started to compose music when we millennials in India were beginning to make memories. His songs are the soundtrack of our childhood. We grew up together; and while decades have passed, his songs continue to be the musical cues that mark the milestones in our journeys.

We have both changed over the years, Rahman's music and we, his listeners – but his music especially has evolved. As in life, the only constant in Rahman's music is change. I don't mind it, I actively want it, but some of these changes are unwelcome. For example, the staggered release of a movie soundtrack album as multiple singles spread over a month, instead of releasing the whole album at once. Though this is an extraneous aspect, external to the music itself, it dilutes the impact and sanctity of a new Rahman album experience.

Releasing singles from an album is akin to clouds breaking as sporadic drizzle rather than as a downpour. I prefer to get sopping wet in the pouring rain. I try to wait until the whole album is out to listen to all the songs in a sequence. It is not just that no two Rahman albums sound the same; no two songs in an album are the same. A Rahman album delivered as singles is like a rainbow showing up one colour at a time.

Every Rahmaniac is caught in a dilemma whenever a single is out – to listen or not to listen. Sometimes I succumb to the temptation. It has become much harder to refrain from hitting the play button now that millions of listeners flood Twitter and Facebook with their ruminations on a song only minutes after it has been released. Sometimes, I listen to the song once; just as a sip to wet the tongue so that I don't die of thirst.

This new romantic song has been released as a single. The complete album release is a few weeks away. I hear the song once. Only once. I couldn't hear it again. I shouldn't hear it again. Not immediately. Not because I want to wait for the whole album, but because I am unable to make myself available as the ideal listener that the song deserves. It calls for a quiet ambience and undivided attention. I haven't been able to make space and time for it yet. I haven't been able to turn off the world around me.

I listen to music every day on my iPod during my hour-long commute to work. I travel by a non-air-conditioned bus. I board the bus at the terminus in the morning, and so every day I get to choose my seat. I prefer a window seat, and take one in the row at the centre of the bus, a spot equidistant from both the front and rear where the bumps in the ride are felt the least. I keep the sliding doors of the window open for ventilation and in barges the noise of the bustling metropolitan city. A journey by public transport

A journey by public transport in Bangalore—a city that was once a pensioner's paradise, now a paradise lost, India's Silicon Valley—is one through a barrage of sounds hammering at your eardrums

in Bangalore – a city that was once a pensioner's paradise, now a paradise lost, India's Silicon Valley – is one through a barrage of sounds hammering at your eardrums: buzzing bus engine, honking vehicles on the road, clamouring passengers, the sound of incessant blabbering of a garrulous radio jockey booming from the cheap, shrill speakers inside the bus. Noise-cancelling headphones cancels little on Bangalore roads.

I unbutton the top two shirt buttons and wipe the sweat off the nape of my neck using my handkerchief. I relax, recline on the Rexine seat, close my eyes and wear my in-ear earpiece. Hitting my face is gushing wind mixed with fine dust that swirls up from the dry tarmac: it makes me sneeze. I swipe the glossy surface of my iPod a few times from top to bottom, left to right; and finally, with a single firm tap I enter the song's universe.

A soft, angelic female voice in a husky tone and musical inflexion says – doesn't sing – three words: '*Hey! Maryan, Vaa.*' (Hey! Maryan, come) She calls for her love, Maryan. It sounds both a command and a request. She asks her man, who has been abducted and is held hostage in a land far, far away, to come back home. Before she can complete the three words, the bus driver applies a shuddering brake; a hasty man from the sidewalk, paying no heed to the stop signal, had crossed the road in front of our fast-approaching bus. The tyres' high-pitched screech fills the deliberate stretches of silence between each spouted word. The jolt pushes my body forward and pulls me rudely out of the song and back into the real world. I switch off my iPod.

And now creeps in the worst of all noises, the voice inside my head: it screams thoughts pertaining to work ... I tick the boxes on a virtual checklist in my mind

I reach my office, an air-conditioned space insulated from the noise of the world outside. Work has been hectic this week. Amidst coding, gossiping, emails, conference calls and meetings, I disappear from my cubicle with my iPod and seek refuge in the toilet. And now creeps in the worst of all noises, the voice inside my head: it screams thoughts pertaining to work. I wonder if I ran all the prerequisite steps for the critical batch job that I will kick-start in a few hours in the production system. I tick the boxes on a virtual checklist in my mind. The song has been playing in a continuous loop. The next iteration is about to begin. I think about the status reports I am yet to prepare, time sheets I have to fill, and the lines of RPG/400 code I have to peer-review before the end of the day. I realise that it has been fifteen minutes since I sat on the toilet and I haven't yet focused on the song. I shake my head, hoping this will help my mind push thought to one side and create a secluded space for music. It doesn't work. So, I sit up straight, lean back on the cistern, take a deep breath and close my eyes. The song gradually calms all my wandering thoughts. Finally, in the toilet, I listen, and I absorb parts of the song.

This is what I hear: the orchestration is dense, but it floats light as if sparse. The delicate melody is wrapped with the choicest of warm tones and textures from many layers of acoustic and electronic instruments. The song segues from one section to another to arrive at the line where the lyricist sets a fantastical scene of romance: a sky that has a hundred moons and a flock of bluebirds flying at random. Here the contour of the melody reaches its romantic summit. I slide along the ebb and flow of the melody. Maryan, the man, is now requesting the vast skies to bring back the past, the time they spent together, to here and now. And the song pauses for a second. Stillness. Silence.

A sudden burst of jarring, comical jazz – a cue from Rahman's score for another Hindi romantic comedy – disrupts the silence. It is my mobile ringtone. My project manager is calling. I answer. He wants me to send the weekly status report immediately. I run to my desk. I didn't get another opportunity to listen to the song again in the workplace.

I come home in the evening. I can't blast the song aloud on my big Bose speakers in the cramped neighbourhood because all the windows in the house are kept open, again, for ventilation. I go to bed. I wear my Apple earphones, and I play the song on my iPod. I can hear my flatmates chatting loudly in the living room; they are watching a cricket match on TV. More noise. I close the door to my room. Then, I hear the ceiling fan that has been set to run at high speed to beat the sultry weather. It produces a loud whirring sound that sneaks through the gap between my ears and the earpiece and becomes an unwelcome accompaniment to the song.

I contemplate moving to the open terrace at the top of our apartment building. No one lingers there at this hour. I might have to tolerate a few stinging mosquitoes, but that is a small price to pay to be able to listen to the song in solitude for a few minutes before I go to sleep.

I go to the terrace. It is still warm outside. I hear the rustle of the leaves in the trees; a slight breeze, but it has no effect on the sweat pearling on my forehead. I return to music, the vroom of the vehicles on the street below stabs at the silences in the song. I retreat further; settling for a corner far from the street and sit on the rough, corrugated floor of the terrace. I play the song on my iPod, plug in my earpiece and focus hard.

I hear the celestial chorus. Those thin, sparkling bell strokes have the whiff of nineties Rahman.

A quiet piano riff is omnipresent, and it pecks at the cheeks of the vocal melody. An almost muted harp glissando acts as a springboard from where leaps the first reprise of the main verse. The sprinklings of accordion pieces around the melody evoke a dreamy, languid aura. The feeble strains of a sarangi appear – a bowed string instrument that buzzes at a pitch close to that of a bee – which agrees with the man, who sings that his girl's voice is sweet as honey. Throughout the song, the backing strings section whirls and stirs, soars and falls, flutters and floats. I hear them. I hear them all. However, something's amiss. It doesn't seem enough. I want to go further and deeper. I want to absorb those nanoseconds of pregnant silence from which the many sonic worlds of the song are born.

A quiet piano riff is omnipresent, and it pecks at the cheeks of the vocal melody. An almost muted harp glissando acts as a springboard from where leaps the first reprise of the main verse

I can't wait to watch the film Maryan – for which this song was written – in the controlled environment of a cinema theatre. For five minutes the entire space will be filled only with the sounds and silences of the song. To quash the noise of the song's visuals, I will close my eyes the moment the song starts to play. I don't want my mind to process any new data apart from that fed by the sound of the music and the music of silence. However, the film's release is several months away. I can't wait that long.

I decide to go home the following weekend, to my parents, to Salem, five hours by bus from Bangalore. In Salem, I can get the space and time I have been craving for.

Friday night. I board a semi-sleeper air-conditioned bus for Salem. The in-bus entertainment is already on: an old Tamil film is playing on a large LCD television screen dangling from the roof beside the driver's seat. The television is connected to multiple speakers placed in the overhead baggage space that runs the length of the

I wake up to find the earphone cable wound around my neck. I scratch my left cheek to find a sleep mark the size and thickness of the earphone cable. The song is still playing

bus. The atonal voice of the film's hero espousing his ideologies echoes inside the bus; it is the worst sonic accompaniment the song that I have been trying to listen to could ever have. I wear an earpiece and try to listen to it, but I can't. It feels disrespectful to hear the song in this environment; I switch off.

I arrive at my parents' home around midnight. After devouring my mother's delicious dosa with coconut chutney, I go to bed. I remove the batteries from the wall clock in the room so that its ticking sound doesn't become a dissonant metronome to the song. At last, I get to hear the music in the ambience I wanted.

The neighbourhood is quiet and asleep, except for the chirp of the lizards crawling across the walls of my room. I switch off the ceiling fan and turn on the air-conditioner; the AC's constant hum much quieter than the fan's mechanical whirr. I push the earpiece as tight as possible into my ears. I play the song and listen mindfully for an hour, and then in a quasi-sleep state for another hour. I hear at once all the intricate instrumental layers of the song I gathered in parts over the past week.

I don't know when I fell asleep. I wake up to find the earphone cable wound around my neck. I scratch my left cheek to find a sleep mark the size and thickness of the earphone cable. The song is still playing.

Now, only now, can I claim to have heard the song. However, I wish I could mute this universe at will – just once, for a few minutes – so I could listen to those sharp nodes of silence that precede the sound. Or, better yet, someone fit me into a space suit with this song and toss me into the cosmos. **H**

Nacional 27

by Nicholas Ward

It was the night before Christmas at the Bar Louie on Chicago Avenue. It's long gone now, like almost everything in this story, replaced by an upscale gastropub. Open until 4am, Bar Louie felt lonely on a good night. That night – morning really – my friends and I should have gone home after work. But we needed a drink; wanted to raise a glass to the end of the year, and the end of something else.

'What time is your train tomorrow?' Luis asked. He would celebrate the holiday with his room-mates, who he knew from Ecuador, many of whom worked in the industry.

'6 am,' I said. I flipped open my phone to check the time. 'Five hours from now.'

'Let's have another,' Jeff said.

He signaled to the bartender, who was slumped over the prep table talking to the grill guy. Jeff's family lived downstate, halfway between Springfield and St. Louis, closer than I lived to my parents' house outside Detroit. He wouldn't go home either.

'Your last night is next week?' Luis asked.

'New Year's Eve,' I said, 'out with a bang.'

'You nervous?' Jeff asked.

I shrugged, a deflection.

Another round of beers arrived and we toasted in the Chicago way: raise the glass in your friends' direction, tap it lightly on the bar top, take a pull.

'You can't do both?' Luis asked.

'It seems too hard,' I said. 'Requesting so many nights off, closing when I have auditions the next morning. If I'm going to take my life seriously, I might as well do it now.'

'I don't get it,' Luis said.

'It's a career move,' Jeff said, 'I'm proud of you.'

'Thank you.' I looked at Luis. 'At least someone understands me.'

We all worked at Nacional 27, a fine-dining restaurant around the corner from Bar Louie. I'd lived in Chicago for little over a year. Jeff and Luis were the first two non-college friends I'd made, the first of that sort that lasted.

For comida, the pre-service staff meal, one of the sous chefs Gustavo cooked roasted plantains, rice and beans, extra suckling pig we'd acquired for dinner service. Everyone ate together before the shift – the cooks, bussers and bartenders, food runners, hosts and servers – all congregated around the long circular bar, as the day faded to dusk.

On that evening, the night before Christmas, we put out a special menu: roasted plantains, rice and beans, suckling pig roasted whole. We weren't busy, slow enough that I still remember my guests. One was a woman and her younger brother. He tried to order a drink. When I asked for ID, she asked, 'You can't make an exception, just for tonight?'

'Wish I could,' I said.

I placed her drink between the both of them, knowing that when they shared it, I'd look the other way. I wondered if their parents were alive, if they were making new rituals. I wondered about my own parents, what they'd say if they knew I'd asked to work this miserable shift.

'The guy is back,' Jeff said. We stood at the entrance to the dining room, a circle of plush black booths with tables in the center and a raised platform beyond. On a busy Saturday, the room exploded with heat. Tonight the space felt cold.

'Dead wife guy?'

Jeff nodded. I looked across the room, at the guest Jeff had served earlier in the week. He was seated at the same four-top, an empty place setting in front of him. A few days before, another slow pre-holiday night, a host of personnel had tried to remove the extra setting but he insisted it stay. He told Jeff that his wife had just passed away and that he wanted to keep the place for her.

'It's your table,' Jeff said. He handed me a chit from the host stand, with the man's name and a note all in caps: LEAVE ONE EXTRA SETTING.

I sighed. 'Today must be really hard for him.'

'Tomorrow is gonna be worse,' Jeff said.

I stumbled over to greet him. I can no longer

remember what he looked like, what he ordered, if I offered my condolences. All I recall is that as I approached him, I adopted a strange loping gait: I realized that I'd split my pants.

Because I was leaving the job, I'd not bothered with uniform maintenance. That had allowed a tiny hole in the taint region of my black dress pants to elongate until I was now forced to walk with clenched buttocks. The sole of my right shoe was nearly detached and flapped on the tiled floor.

I wondered if their parents were alive, if they were making new rituals. I wondered about my own parents, what they'd say if they knew I'd asked to work this miserable shift

After work, I tried to use my wardrobe malfunctions as an excuse not to go out. I was downstairs putting on my overcoat when Luis cornered me in the break area.

'Beers?' he asked. He leaned on the door of the locker room. He looked like a model with his coiffed black hair.

'I have an early train,' I said.

'You don't need to be sober for that,' he said. A fair argument.

'Man, my pants are split from ass to cock and my fucking shoe has a hole in it.'

'No one cares,' he said. 'We need to make use of our time together.'

I relented, like he knew I would. 'Is anything even open?' I asked.

I'd begun working at Nacional 27 on the corner of Huron and Orleans streets in the winter of 2004. A restaurant that transformed into a nightclub on weekends, the place enthralled me. It occupied the ground floor of a seven-story office block visible from the Brown Line. One side of the building was decorated with a large ad for the restaurant; a woman's leg protruding from her nightgown in mid-dance stride. The image had been plastered directly onto the bricks. It gave the appearance of something cracked, something worn and nostalgic. Inside, cream-colored curtains nestled the free-standing bar, liquor bottles stacked to the ceiling. It looked how I thought a Havana nightclub might have appeared, before Communism. I was familiar with family diners, sports bars, national chains and white tablecloths for special occasions. Nacional was in a different solar system.

Like most of the staff, I was often in some state of dishevelment: hungover, unshowered or surly. Most times all three

I interviewed there twice, in two different rounds of job searches.

'Why do you want to work here so badly?' Jay, the manager, asked on my second interview, after I'd spent a few months at the old Cy's Crabhouse on Ashland Avenue.

'Look around,' I said. 'This place is sexy. I want to be a part of that.'

I'd waited tables since high school, first at the family restaurant Bill Knapps, then at a small bed and breakfast in Oxford, Ohio. The Alexander House was upscale but it was still a college town. We free-poured drinks and served chops with a minimum of plating. The chef offered some adventurous forays, a calamari fritto misto, a lavash cracker for flatbreads. Like most of the staff, I was often in some state of dishevelment: hungover, unshowered or surly. Most times all three. In Chicago, at Nacional 27, I started to take seriously the craft of working in a restaurant.

Colorful and vibrant, the menu mixed spice and savory and sweet into an array of flavors and textures. There were plantain croquettes, BBQ-d lamb, tiny tacos, ahi tuna and watermelon ceviche, shrimp adobado, tender pork confit, and beef tenderloin medallions topped with a chimichurri crust. The wine list boasted hundreds of bottles, 27 of them under $27, the big boys topping out at 300 bucks. I drank malbecs and cameneres and petit verdots for the first time. The cocktail program spun classics like mojitos, caipirinhas, and pisco sours, alongside inventions like El Corazon, tequila with pomegranate and a hint of spice on the rim.

We didn't serve chips and guacamole. 'We're not a Mexican restaurant,' Chef Randy informed me. 'There's nothing wrong with chips and guac, but we're concerned with everything south of North America.'

Bald with thin-framed spectacles, Randy Zweiban was from Queens but had spent decades under the famed Florida chef, Norman Van Aken, who cooked what he called 'New World cuisine', a mash-up of Latin, Caribbean, African, and American flavors. Van Aken claimed to have invented the idea of 'fusion' with regards to food. Randy kept more to the mainland (plus Cuba), working in the Nuevo Latino tradition, a different but related culinary expression. The guiding principle was that the United States had smashed together the people of Central and South America and that they had naturally begun to exchange and share cultures and flavors with one another. We saw ourselves as stewards of this cuisine and delivered the news with aplomb. How amazing, that Nicaraguan people ended up in Omaha. How delightful, to project the sun-caked images of *The Motorcycle Diaries* on the wall. How delicious, the food this mashing of people has provided us.

Looking back, with the knowledge I didn't have then, this positive spin makes a kind of capitalist sense, even if I cringe at it. Explaining our cuisine through the lens of colonialism, imperialism, the transatlantic slave trade, Native American genocide, CIA-backed assassinations and neoliberal US policy wouldn't exactly excite our guests to indulge. Randy held a deep love for the food he cooked and the people who helped inspire it. His leadership kept Nacional singular, even though he never learned Spanish. Indeed, when Randy finally left to start his own restaurant, the corporate overlords at Lettuce Entertain You put chips and guac on the menu, opened a section of the restaurant as a taco stand and never replaced him with another executive chef.

By the time I started working at Nacional, I'd

lived in Chicago for four months. That time felt endless to me: four months of wandering, working a job I hated; four months of waiting, always waiting, for my life to start. Nacional changed that in an instant. I was on fire with the world. My first night on the floor, after two weeks of training, I got along so well with my final table that when I saw them across the street at the Green Door Tavern, they bought me a drink to celebrate my first successful night as a fine-dining server in the city of Chicago.

Luis started a few months after I did. He was tense. He sought a life in restaurants and connected his trajectory to this first opportunity with a fine-dining Lettuce Entertain You restaurant. Such was the power of the group: once you were in, you were golden forever. Anxiety clouded Luis' judgment, it wrecked his ability to learn and translate the menu to his guests, and subverted his grace under pressure. One of his first nights, he ran afoul of Randy. It was a busy Saturday and he'd screwed up a bunch of orders. Randy pulled Jay and the other manager aside and told them he wanted Luis fired. The managers pivoted, sent Luis home, and told him to return the next night knowing the menu back and front. They tasked me with taking over the tables in his section.

'You saved my career,' Luis once said to me, much later. I waved the compliment away. 'No, you did,' he insisted, 'if you don't take my section, I get fired and who knows where I'll be today.' Luis studied the menu and aced his test. He became a manager at Nacional 27, hired me twice more in my serving career and is now the Director of Operations for a gigantic hospitality conglomerate in Denver.

Luis drove everywhere. My roommates and I had access to cars, but we always took the train if we could help it. Not Luis. After work, we'd climb into his VW bug and zip to his favorite bars in the city. Luis favored dumb sports bars in bro-y neighborhoods. He didn't even like sports. He never blended in to bro culture. But his favorite bar was a slab-of-concrete hellhole near his apartment in Lakeview called Tai's Til 4. We'd stumble in after 2 am, drunk but cogent, and watch blackout types fall over each other. I wondered about the bartenders, what kind of debauchery they witnessed on a nightly basis, what the bar looked like after all the drunks left, vomit and piss and sexual fluids all over the place.

One such Saturday in the summer, this new guy with funky hair joined us for a night out. When offered a ride, he declined, saying instead that he'd brought his bike along.

'You bike that far?' I asked; we were standing outside a bar in Lincoln Park.

Jeff shook his head. 'It's not that far,' he said.

When we pulled up to Tai's and piled out, there he was, pulling up to the curb. Jeff was the first person I knew to ride a bike in Chicago, an activity I now prefer as my main mode of transit. A few nights later, I was humming a song while making coffee in the kitchen. Jeff cruised past me on a different mission. 'Tom Waits?' he asked.

'It is,' I said, 'you like Tom Waits?'

'I love him.'

That sealed our friendship. Jeff was a music obsessive and we bonded over the latest releases. It felt good to have a friend like this, someone with whom I could share my interests. Towards the end of the holidays, Jeff gave me a mix CD with his favorite songs from that year.

The three of us became inseparable, inside the restaurant and without. We pounded beers after work and followed Luis to his favorite shit holes

The three of us became inseparable, inside the restaurant and out. We pounded beers after work and followed Luis to his favorite shit holes. One Sunday night we blew our whole take on a fancy dinner at Smith and Wollensky overlooking the Chicago river. It was the night the White Sox made the World Series. A few days later, when Jeff's beloved Astros did too, I joined him for celebration drinks.

Nacional put me inside a tension I lived with for years. I'd moved to Chicago to be an actor. I told myself to audition at a fever pitch, to really go after my life with all the tenacity I could muster. But at Nacional, I found a vital space where I could meet people, make friends, learn about food and wine – and make more money than I ever thought possible. Each night on the floor was its own mini-play, with servers and managers and runners and bussers and bartenders who dazzled the audience, with a whole host of craftspeople backstage, pulling levers the crowd didn't know existed. I loved that action.

The rituals held it all together. Before each shift,

the whole staff ate together – the cooks, bussers and bartenders, food runners, hosts and servers. We sat at Table 81, the semi-private round table up the ramp from the DJ booth, reserved for large parties. Over comida, we'd talk shit, mostly at each other, sometimes about the guests we'd had the night before, a just-OK restaurant that we'd visited the week before, or just bullshit; talk about the weather, politics, sports, movies. Once finished eating, pre-shift started, the time for the chef and managers to run through the night's activities; make us aware of the specials or any important guests.

The tasks were tedious but paramount. If we hadn't finished those items before the guests piled in, the night could go down in flames

Occasionally they'd offer tips sent down from corporate. We always hated those, some suit trying to tell us how to up-sell a few additional sides, to boost our check and the corporation's coffers. I liked the period between pre-shift and the start of dinner service, with each server and busser assigned daily tasks: folding napkins, stocking plates and glasses, polishing the silverware until it sparkled just so. A mixture of English and Spanish, shit-talking the real language, vulgar and offensive, an HR department's nightmare.

'Hola pincha Nick,' Jesus, one of the bussers, would sing, sliding a tray of polished knives into the side station, while I folded napkins into our singular tri-fold. The tasks were tedious but paramount. If we hadn't finished those items before the guests piled in, the night could go down in flames.

By far the best part of the job – of any serving job – was talking to the guests. Nacional started me on a path of loving food, of trying to understand food. Pushing that excitement out into the world was easy. Over time, I learned how to read a table: to guide the guests that really wanted my input, to back off from those who required space, to change my inflection based on their energy, to know when to push them for that extra drink. I learned how to describe our restaurant with tenderness and vitality, to showcase its sexiness. I learned that a good server is a tour guide and a magician, that they spin guests through the experience and anticipate their needs before they themselves even know what they want. When they leave – happy, intoxicated and love-drunk, having spent money they didn't even know they had and waving away their concerns for a few hours, an extra 'thank-you' piled on top of that big fat tip – that was the real action.

Every Friday and Saturday at 11pm the entire restaurant transformed. Tables were whisked away from the center of the dining room, the large centerpiece containing stacks of carefully inlaid glasses and trays of silverware was wheeled off to an undisclosed location, and suddenly we had a dance floor. The bar swelled with an influx of people, regulars who came each week to our club, and new arrivals curious about our Latin beats. Each week, the same song kicked us off, a booming bass thundered from the speakers, and we coalesced into a very hot, very sweaty, often-packed Chicago nightclub.

These transitions exhausted me. If I closed, in other words working the nightclub after my serving shift, I became a cocktail waiter, ferrying trays of drinks back and forth. But the pathway from the bar to the dance floor was often blocked, so most nights I'd have to go all the way around, into one door of the kitchen and out the other side. It took twenty minutes to land drinks on tables, something guests were never fond of. It was pulsating and chaotic and the patrons were boorish. So far removed from the tenderness of one hour prior. And since I was trying to get my acting career off the ground, it wasn't uncommon to work until 3 in the morning with a 9 am audition. If I didn't have an audition, probably I'd stay up until 5 or 6, and then my whole precious Sunday was shot.

One night, Jesus dropped an entire tray's worth of glasses he'd just cleared from a nine-top. It was during the transition, while throngs of people attempted to pass from the bar to the club.

Perhaps he had packed it too full, but this was understandable. He wanted to get it all out of the way asap. Shattered glass covered the floor, a team of staff rushed over to help clean it up, while others made space for this to be done.

'Who's going to pay for my dry-cleaning?': a white guy, slacks and a striped shirt.

I spun around on him. 'Fuck your dry cleaning, we need to make sure this is safe.'

He protested.

'Go to the host stand, get a card from the manager.'

Enough nights were like this, combative outbursts between guests and sometimes co-workers, that I coiled myself in anxiety and anger and felt like I needed the release of four to six beers and a cab ride home. I hadn't yet learned to let the muck of the job roll off my back.

> **I coiled myself in anxiety and anger and felt like I needed the release of four to six beers and a cab ride home. I hadn't yet learned to let the muck of the job roll off my back**

With hindsight, it wasn't the restaurant. I couldn't figure out my relationship to my own life. I wanted the thrill of the job and I wanted to pursue my dreams. I didn't think I could have it both ways. I got into my head that I couldn't maintain a relationship with this restaurant, any restaurant, and still have a theatre career. At the time, that's all I wanted. This is maybe the whitest thing about me, that I could have a good job surrounded by people I enjoyed, in pursuit of something we all made together and feel like it wasn't enough.

Or maybe this is singular to me. Recently Jeff told me about a conversation he'd had with Luis.

'One night, he and I were standing out back having a smoke and Luis asked: "Have you ever considered doing this as a career?" At that point I hadn't ever. I thought this was a temporary thing and someday I'm gonna get my shit together.'

Jeff also went on to manage Nacional and then Randy's next restaurant, Province, before opening a series of very successful bars and starting his own hospitality company.

I announced myself one night in early December. I was in the office, turning in my cash on my way out the door.

'Jay,' I said with a dramatic sweep of a hand. 'I need to give two weeks. I just got too much theatre stuff going.'

I concluded with a deft bow. If I expected a ticker-tape parade, Jay shrugged.

'Sounds good,' he said. 'How's New Year's Eve for your last night?'

If that's your life path, you have in front of you a series of small triumphs, near misses, Pyrrhic victories, soft regrets and failures that might look like success

I wasn't being offered the moon. I'd just completed the run of a play, a small storefront Shakespeare production. Another company, a bigger one, wanted my services as an understudy, which I assumed to be a huge honor (it wasn't). I auditioned at every opportunity. I thought I was approaching the precipice, that moment when I would step from one life into the next, from the heady boyhood days of working in restaurants to the grand life of the stage. I didn't believe that I was destined for greatness, only that I was ready to take the next step. But there is no one 'next step', not if you're an artist, or hell, even if you're after a career in hospitality. If that's your life path, you have in front of you a series of small triumphs, near misses, Pyrrhic victories, soft regrets and failures that might look like success. Of course, I didn't know that at the time.

'Where shall we go?' Luis asked. We stood outside Nacional's revolving doors. It had begun to rain, lightly, turning soft snow into slush. I wiggled my toes. They were a little wet already.

We looked at The Green Door Tavern, closed for the night. Built, they say, on the rubble of the Chicago fire, with a slanted roof to prove it, Green Door was our favorite bar. That's where we wanted to drink, but we were happy for Paulie and his crew to have closed early for the holiday.

'Blue Frog?' Jeff suggested.

'You think there's gonna be karaoke tonight?' Luis asked.

'You never know,' Jeff said.

We set off, the streets of the neighborhood quiet. A Brown Line rumbled over our heads. It was still shy of 11, but the town felt deserted, like we'd stumbled into the pre-dawn.

'Luis, you don't have a hat?' I asked.

He pointed to his black hair, short but swooping across his head.

'You think I want to ruin this with a hat?' he asked.

At the Blue Frog, now defunct, closed by developers like most of the great bars in Chicago, Jeff ran to the front door, which was set a few paces back from the street.

'How's your foot?' Luis asked.

'Squishy,' I said. 'I need a drink to warm up.'

We watched Jeff peer into the bar's windows. No lights were on.

'You're gonna temp?' Luis asked.

'That's the plan,' I said.

'You have experience in an office?'

'Nope,' I said and we both laughed.

'They're closed,' Jeff said. 'Clark Street?'

This was 2005. We couldn't take out our smart phones and check to see if they were open, or even pull up their numbers and call ahead. We trudged on, past the flower shop on LaSalle where, if you looked south, you could see all the way to the Chicago Board of Trade, towards the Clark Street Ale House, fine purveyors of high alcohol beers. They were closed too.

I knew I would stay in that moment forever. That whatever I did with my life, whomever I became, I'd carry that night with me

'I'm calling it a night,' I said.

Luis and Jeff protested.

'Noooo, come on, we gotta buy you a drink.'

'Guys, I'm tired, my foot is soaked, my pants are split from ass to cock, I can barely walk.'

Luis held up a finger. 'One more,' he said. 'We'll try one more.' It wasn't a question.

We turned west on Chicago Avenue, on our way to completing a loop around the neighborhood. The wide street glistened in the rain, the garish lights of the gas station hung hazy, cars hissing as they drove the wet streets, maybe headed home, or maybe somewhere we couldn't fathom, somewhere they too could pretend it wasn't a sacred night.

'The dead wife guy say anything to you?' Jeff asked.

'No,' I said. 'I was too nervous to talk to him. I didn't know what to say.'

'You gotta have empathy,' Luis said.

'I have empathy,' I said. 'But he's not my dad or my cousin or anything.'

'You still need to have empathy,' Luis said. 'That's the job.'

We were quiet. Something about the lights, the sounds of the cars, my squishy foot, the banter with my two friends, talk of death, of finding a beer to drink the night before Christmas, I knew I would stay in that moment forever. That whatever I did with my life, whomever I became, I'd carry that night with me.

'Bar Louie?' I asked. We'd stopped across the street, near the entrance to the L. The bar chain's sign was lit up, a few candles flickering in the window.

'I hate that place,' Jeff said.

'Me too,' Luis said.

'Well, it's the only spot open, so if you want a beer, let's get a beer,' I said.

We looked at each other, shrugged our shoulders, and crossed the street in the rain. **H**

This is not a
ghost story

but a haunting

by Katie Simpson

▪ Haunt (v) – to continually seek the company of

All definitions taken from Merriam-Webster,
https://www.merriam-webster.com/dictionary/haunt

My mother finds ancestors echoing in my body. My toes are my Aunt Rebecca's. My hair is the same color as my father's. I wear my paternal grandfather's face.

When I am 13, my mother starts to say I have my grandmother Ann's hips. While my mother's weight falls behind her, mine falls forward. My body, apple shaped, is returning to the tree.

I begin to stare at myself in front of the mirror, trying to see my grandmother. Dying when my mother was just 23, the only source I have is my mother's memory.

In my early twenties, my mother decides it's time to pass on some of her jewelry. We sit by the safe as she pulls each piece out. Bags and boxes surround us on the floor, an assortment of heirlooms and pieces she no longer wears. My eyes are attracted to the old ones: a set of golden clover earrings and matching bracelet; the garnet cuff. Each time, she admits they were my grandmother's.

'I'm not ready.' My mother says each time, moving them aside.

She gives me one ring. It's a gold band with a small abstract brown painting on an opal-like stone. I've never seen anything like it. Now, I wear it every day. My mother says it makes her happy but her smile never reaches her eyes.

—

My grandmother Ann hated pictures. She didn't like how she looked in them despite her oval face, smooth skin and warm brown eyes.

A few have survived, including a professional portrait in black and white. It sits in a silver frame. Beneath the glass, my grandmother poses, her dark coiffed hair setting off her pale skin.

I can never just glance at it. I stare and wonder. When talking to the photographer, did she speak with the broad 'A's of Boston? When they finished the photograph, did her hand itch to pull out a cigarette?

Now I purposely skip over the image, afraid of my fictions becoming memory.

Haunt (v) – Be persistently and disturbingly present in (the mind)

My various names: Katheryn Anne Simpson, when I've upset my mother; Chanah, in Jewish ritual; Katie Anne, on Facebook.

Anne, an homage to my grandmother. A silent 'e' to tell me apart. But when they call me, her name echoes. Like an incantation, we speak spells in a language almost forgotten.

I am amazed at Jewish mourning rituals because they acknowledge the length and distance of grief. The beginning is intense. For the first seven days we sit on floors, covering mirrors, letting the community hold us.

After a week, we return to work but are in Sheloshim, for 30 days. We don't cut our hair or go to celebrations. Mourning officially lasts a year. We chant Kaddish every day. Slowly, we are brought from grief into life.

Even once the year ends, we still make moments for mourning. There is the Yahrzeit, or the death anniversary, where we stand again as mourners. There is Yizkor, a special service to remember the dead on Passover, Sukkot, Shavuot and Yom Kippur.

Life goes on, but grief never ends.

Haunt (n) – to have a disquieting or harmful effect on: TROUBLE

My Hebrew name, Chanah, comes from the biblical character, Hannah. She is childless and one day goes to the temple to pray.

God grants her wish and Hannah bears a son, Samuel. Just after weaning him, she returns to the temple and offers the boy to become a priest. Research tells us that he couldn't have been more than four years-old.

On my mother's 40th birthday, I am holding her together. She's crying because of something her father has yelled at her. As I sit with my mother, my eyes focus on the Persian rug; intricacies laced through the red weave. I pick up patterns quickly, whether it's a rug or my mother's sorrow. My eight-year-old hands pat her cheek, grasping for her elegant fingers.

When my mother is three years-old, her hands are steady enough to pour orange juice for my grandmother. At five, her hands can rub icing across my grandmother's gums. Before she can read chapter books, she can identify the pattern of diabetes and sugar levels.

A difference of 33 years disappears in our hands. Our eyes seek the signs; our hands shoot out, trying to catch you.

In Lacanian psychoanalysis, the Oedipal Complex becomes metaphorical. The child is trying to understand what the mother wants and then seeks to become that 'fully satisfying love-object.' Unless the child is thwarted, they will remain, 'trying to fathom and fulfil this desire.'

Origin of the word haunt: Middle English, from Anglo-French hanter, probably from Old Norse heimta to lead home, pull, claim, from heimr home

My grandmother lived for over two decades in the DC area, but I remember her most at my great-grandmother Gordon's house in Marblehead, Massachusetts. It was where she took her two daughters – my mother and aunt – during the summer, a time of sunshine and space from a broken marriage.

When I was young, my mother took me there too. The house looked the same. The living room was still dark brown paneling, the bathroom bright pink tile. As my brother and I played by the water, my mother would sit with my great-grandmother. How easy it could've been to believe my grandmother Ann was also there, just around the corner.

In my twenties, the seaside haven began to crumble. The details of my grandmother's almost-divorce are hazy. What is vivid: a woman flies to New England with a newborn. She turns to her parents for solace. Her parents shake their heads. They tell her to return to the man who bruises her shoulders.

He is her home now.

My grandmother is buried just a few miles from the New England sea. She rests with her parents in the Gordon family plot. I don't worry about her, despite the harsh winter. She lies in a safe space.

▎Haunt (v.i) – to stay around or persist : LINGER

When my family talks about my grandmother, we can't avoid the conditional perfect tense. She would've been happier if she'd left him. If she hadn't had diabetes, she wouldn't have been so vulnerable. If she hadn't undergone experimental surgery to recover her eyesight, she would have lived longer.

Even my mother's certainty (she would've loved you) remains in the conditional.

The tense seeds doubt. What would our relationship have looked like? Would she have loved my intersectional feminism, my biting tongue, the tattoo of poetry stanzas or my uneven chipped nails?

> She would've adored you.
> She would've reveled in your mind.
> She would've loved you.

But we can't escape these conditions.

There are days when I'm swallowed in her coda. My travel around the world is her late freedom. My stubborn tongue whips back against her husband's barbs. In these moments, I want to ask Ann so many things. Show me what is yours, so I can find what is mine. But there is only silence.

In that silence, I return to what I know. We're not a novel or a prophecy, just a family caught in time. She is always behind me. I am always ahead. Even with her hips, her blood, the only story I can write is my own. **H**

{papermash}

www.papermash.co.uk

National Newark and Essex

by Roger Conant Cranse

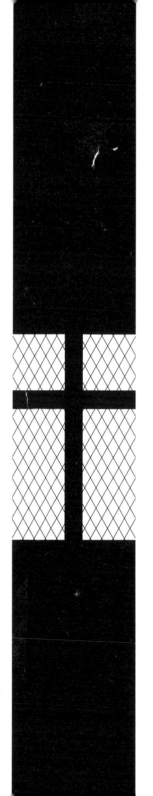

In the summer of 1956, Dwight D. Eisenhower was running for his second term and *Why Do Fools Fall in Love?* by Frankie Lymon & the Teenagers had hit the top ten. I was 15 years old and had just started my first indoor job, working for Eisenhower's re-election. I was the office boy at the New Jersey Republican Finance Committee on the 27th floor of the National Newark and Essex, a pyramidal heap that rose up thirty-five floors to dominate the Newark skyline. I'd earned $3.50 a week in my previous job as a paperboy; this office boy job paid $1.25 an hour – in those days Republicans knew value when they saw it.

The National Newark and Essex was served by sixteen elevators, eight on each side of a wide bay in the middle of the building. Eleven years after the end of the Second World War, order still mattered in the country. A uniformed captain stationed in the center of the bay brought system to the morning rush. Only one of the sixteen cars filled at a time. The captain pointed a rigid arm to this car. His other arm swung pendulum-like, herding people into it. When the elevator filled up, the captain lifted his arm in a halt sign, snapped his fingers and barked, 'Hut!' The door of the elevator closed instantly, the captain marched five paces along the gleaming terrazzo floor to the next vacant elevator and directed the troops towards it. The operators waiting their turn to be called to action stood at parade rest in front of their cars. By the time the last elevator was dispatched upwards the first had returned from the top of the building to refill for another trip.

An operator actually drove his car using a lever set in a polished brass control panel next to the door. He stood with his back to the control panel, facing into the car as it filled up. Passengers moved to the back of the car, turned, and called out their floors: 'Seven, please,' 'Six,' 'Twenty-four.' Of course, the operator knew the regulars and their floors. In those cases there was a series of good mornings: 'Good morning, John.' 'Good morning, sir. Good morning, ma'am.' When the command came – 'Hut!' – the operator reached over, grasped a jointed bar, and shut the floor's steel door. He then closed the car's grated door, designed much like a child protective gate.

After closing the doors the operator fell back into position facing his passengers, reached behind and moved the driving lever sideways. The elevator lifted gently, the operator eased the lever farther sideways, the car gathered speed and whizzed upward through the building. The operator looked over his shoulder as the floor numbers flew by on the steel doors. As we approached the first stop, the operator eased the lever toward the upright, the car slowed, crept upward, and stopped. A good operator usually hit the floor exactly. Sometimes, of course, the elevator was a little above or below level and the operator had to bump-

A good operator usually hit the floor exactly. Sometimes the elevator was a little above or below level and the operator had to bump-bump the car with his lever until the floors matched

bump the car with his lever until the floors matched. He then bent sideways, pulled the gate back, levered the steel door open and the passengers marched off to their fate. The operator leaned out to the hallway, announced, 'Going up,' waited a second and a half for passengers, closed the door, closed the gate, turned back to face his passengers and jogged the lever sideways. Of course, the elevator operator could stop the car wherever he wanted.

The country at that time understood order and discipline. People dressed properly. Everyone fell in line. You followed the captain's orders, marched to the designated car, went to the back, faced forward, called out your floor. All this was deeply satisfying to a boy entering the adult world.

My boss was a woman named Doris at the New Jersey Republican Finance Committee. At 15, I divided people age-wise into three groups: kids, grown-ups, and old people. Doris fitted in the middle category. Now, looking back fifty years, I would guess she was in her thirties. I would guess she turned men's heads on the street. At the time I only noticed her hair: short, dark, with white flecks all over, something like chicken feathers. I couldn't figure out what the flecks were; I'd never seen anything like it. I stared. Was it some kind of hair deformity? Was it turning gray in patches? Splattered paint from a weekend project? Doris set me up at a long table in the front room. She explained I'd be assembling packets for county chairmen, ward chairmen and block workers. Each kind of packet was different so I had to pay attention. And I had to be sure to include a gold-colored "IKE" pin in every manila envelope: county, ward, block.

'Every packet, Roger, every packet. People love these pins.'

Doris herself, I noticed, wore a lot of necklaces and rings but never an 'IKE' pin. When these packets were assembled, she told me that I was to pack them in cardboard boxes, seal those boxes, label them, take them down in the elevator to the post office, and ship them.

'OK,' I said, looking at her head. She ran red fingernails through the white flecks.

'If you need help, come in here.' she pointed at an office near the long table. 'Anytime. I live here.'

Then she laughed in a way that said I couldn't possibly understand the joke.

The shipping part of my job took me to the elevator bank often, four or five times a day, and I got to know most of the operators. Some were impassive, regarding an office boy as a kind of gnat that flitted through the building on pesky chores. Others said, 'Hi,' and were nominally friendly. One in particular was kind to the little office boy. He asked how I was doing, talked about how hot Newark was in the summer, and once showed me how he could turn off the light in the car. He reached behind and flicked a switch on the brass panel. Utter darkness swallowed the space, then he flicked again and light sprang up as we sank into the lobby.

And that's how it happened. One torpid afternoon he was taking me up to 27 from a shipping run. I got sleepy in the afternoons then – I still do – and had another two hours of collating, boxing, sealing, labeling, and shipping before I could go home. I was sleepy, he smiled and said, 'Hi.' I said, 'Hi.' He reached over and closed the door and then the gate. We started up, just he and I. The car stopped before we got to 27. I looked up. The blank wall of the elevator shaft showed through the gate. He smiled again, looking down at me. He reached behind. The light went off, everything went black. There was a step, a movement. I felt his breath on my face. And then what I really felt were my cock and balls grabbed and squeezed. Hard. I leapt back and pushed away his hand and summoned all the eloquence of a Jersey boy raised at mid-century.

'Fuck! You fuck!' I shouted. 'Get the fuck out of here!'

The light went on instantly. The man's eyes shone with fear. He was back at the control panel. His mouth pulled tight over his teeth. He started the car.

'I'm sorry, I'm sorry,' he said. The car gained speed. The palm of his hand, raised in supplication, pleaded with me.

'You fucking bastard,' I shouted and strode out at 27.

'Don't tell anyone,' he said as I passed through the doors.

'Are you OK?' Doris looked over her shoulder. I'd begun packing a block worker's box.

I saw him one more time ... We weren't alone. His mouth twitched into a scared smile. I acted like he wasn't there. And then he wasn't

'Yeah, I'm OK,' I said, squeezing a folder into the end of the box.

I told her the next morning.

'We'll take care of it,' she said. 'Don't worry. You were right to tell me, Roger.' I left her office and began collating ward chairman packets. I heard Doris dialing and speaking quietly.

I saw him one more time going down for lunch. We weren't alone. His mouth twitched into a scared smile. I acted like he wasn't there.

And then he wasn't. He'd disappeared. He was gone. Forever. That fucking cocksucker.

Anyway, it didn't matter. I was 15, I knew about queers and homos, I could take care of myself. And besides, it wasn't the first time. The first time was much earlier, when I was very young. I didn't know anything and I couldn't take care of myself.

Back then, when I was 8 years-old, I had begun to attend Bible school with Teddy Hanson, my school friend from down the block. It was his idea. He asked me if I wanted to go to Bible school with him. Teddy was my friend; I asked my parents, they said 'All right, Roger.'

I don't know why they agreed, though. My father never went to church. He told me later that when he was young his parents took him to a Baptist church. The minister had preached that my father would go to hell if he didn't something-or-other – didn't confess, didn't behave right, didn't something. So why they let me go to Bible school, I don't know.

Maybe my mother said, 'It can't do any harm and it's so nice that Roger gets along with the Hanson boy.' And then, maybe, 'If he doesn't like it, we can stop.'

So we went, Teddy and me. The Bible school was in a nice, big house a mile from where we lived. The house had a long porch along the front and down one side. In nice weather we did activities on the porch, like the one where all the boys and girls lined up in single file, bent our arms at the elbows and held onto the elbows of the kid in front. Then we'd repeat 'Choo, choo, choo,' and move our arms back and forth like the driving rods on a steam engine's wheels. We sang songs together and listened to people read the Bible. It was fun.

The school was run by two men who looked exactly alike; you couldn't tell one from the other. I figured it out though: they were twins. Teddy said so too. The twins were very white and soft and pasty-looking. Their bellies curved out like pillows and flopped over big belt buckles carved with pictures. They wore string ties that rested like rats' tails on their bellies. They bent down to talk to you in voices soft as cats' fur.

We went to Bible school once a week after school. Every week after singing and playing choo-choo they moved us to a room where they read the Bible. We sat in rows and after the Bible reading some of the kids – most of the kids – would go around the room saying when they took Jesus into their hearts. They would give the date. 'I took Jesus into my heart December 3, 1948.'

Every week the same kids said the same thing: 'I took Jesus into my heart June 30, 1947.' ... They were so sure, as if they were saying, 'It's raining out'

How did they know? I mean, even the date! I just had no idea. 'Take Jesus into your heart.' What did it mean?

Every week the same kids said the same thing: 'I took Jesus into my heart June 30, 1947.' Or, 'I took Jesus into my heart February 28, 1948.' They were so sure, as if they were saying, 'It's raining out,' or 'I went to Hoboken on the train.' And it was scary too, it made me feel sick in the stomach, like when I got car sick on trips with my parents. 'I took Jesus.' Maybe I didn't want to take Jesus. Or maybe if I didn't take Jesus – 'accept' Jesus, they also said – maybe I was stupid or bad. I just knew I hated that room where they went around every week saying that stuff. Teddy and I were new so we didn't have to say it; we just sat there. And just sitting there not saying anything felt bad too, like you weren't as good or smart as the kids who had taken Jesus into their hearts. They had something you didn't, and they were proud of it and mean because you didn't. I wanted to get out of that room and never go to that place again.

Then one day, when we were getting ready to go home, one of the twins bent down. His cheeks smelled of perfume and when he talked it was like upchuck right in your face

Then one day, when we were getting ready to go home, one of the twins bent down. His cheeks smelled of perfume and when he talked it was like upchuck right in your face. He put his arms over our shoulders.

'Roger and Teddy, next week I want you boys to tell us you've accepted Jesus into your hearts.' His fingers squeezed beside my neck so it hurt. 'OK, boys? You know Jesus loves you.' He squeezed again and I scrunched my shoulders to make him stop. 'Jesus loves you each, Roger and Teddy, very much.' Double squeeze. I tried to twist away. 'Please accept Jesus' love, boys, next week, for Jesus' sake, and yours.' He gave a final pinch and stood up.

We waited outside for Teddy's mom to pick us up. Teddy said, 'I accepted Jesus last week. I just didn't say anything.'

I looked at his face. He didn't look back but his face was so sure. I looked down at my sneakers. How could Teddy do that? I thought he was like me, that he didn't have any idea what taking Jesus into your heart meant. How did he suddenly know? I had wanted to talk to him, I thought he'd understand and that I would feel better.

Could I talk to my parents? 'Mom, Dad, I have to say I accept Jesus into my heart, with the date too.'

No. They'd get mad. I'd feel awful.

So I tried. I prayed.

'Jesus,' I said, kneeling beside my bed, hands folded together in a knot at my chin. 'Jesus…' but then I didn't know what to say after that. There was such complete silence. I think perhaps I was waiting for Jesus to respond, like people did on the telephone. I was waiting for a 'Yeah' from Jesus, or a 'How you doin', Rog?' Or maybe even a nonverbal sign, a feather touch on my shoulder, rustling at the curtains. But there was nothing. Nothing at all.

I felt sick. I didn't want to go back to that awful school. I couldn't quit, though, because on Thursday Teddy's mom would come in their station wagon and I'd have to get in and the station wagon would take us to Bible school and I'd have to go inside. Then I'd be there and the man would come over and lean down and touch me and breathe upchuck on me and hurt my neck. To quit I'd have to tell my parents and they'd get mad. Quitting was bad because you were a quitter, a louse. You gave up. You slunk away. You made your parents sad. Kids hated you.

I tried harder. I ignored the silence. I tried to have feelings for Jesus, love feelings, like the feeling

I had for my cat, Fluffy. I did believe He – Jesus – was up there despite His unresponsiveness. I mean, everyone believed in Jesus and knew Jesus was there, so I did too. Then I figured – OK, all the people in the world, it would be difficult for Him to respond instantly. So I waited. And I began to think, all the people in the world, how could He possibly, possibly even hear them all?

Just a few years earlier I had figured out that Santa couldn't fly to every house in the world – or even the United States – in one night. Impossible. And the houses didn't all have chimneys that led to fireplaces beside Christmas trees. Our house, for example, didn't have a fireplace; the chimney led right to the furnace. I went down to the basement and examined the furnace door. It was small with Duo-Therm written across it and a big iron bar you lifted to open it. Santa couldn't possibly lift the bar from the inside and anyway he'd be burned up before he could try. So the whole Santa business was just impossible, a trick grown-ups played on kids.

But Jesus wasn't. Everyone knew Jesus was up in heaven with God. So I thought of Fluffy. How I loved to pick up Fluffy and put my face in his hair. I tried to transfer that feeling to Jesus in heaven as a way of taking Him into my heart. But it didn't work. I didn't feel anything.

'Jesus, Jesus,' I prayed, 'I take you into my heart.' I pressed my fists to where my heart was. Nothing. I tried to visualize my heart, red, heart-shaped, something going into it, as if through a door, or maybe like putting your hand into water. Nothing. I had no feeling whatsoever for taking Jesus into my heart.

The day came. I woke up and felt sick. I tried one more time. Lying in bed, looking right up at the ceiling toward heaven, looking right to where Jesus was, I imagined Him looking down at me with a kindly, loving expression on His beautiful, thin face. Long, golden hair over His shoulders.

I clenched my hands and said, 'Jesus, I take you into my heart today, now.' Then I got right up and went to the bathroom without thinking. But I knew: nothing.

I clenched my hands and said, 'Jesus, I take you into my heart today, now.' Then I got right up and went to the bathroom without thinking. But I knew: nothing

Teddy's mother arrived in the station wagon; we got out at the school, played choo-choo, then went into the big room. Teddy went first. First timers had to stand all alone in the middle of the room facing the other kids and the twin men. Even at that age – we must have been seven or eight – Teddy had a voice lower than most kids'.

In his low voice, with great surety, he said, 'I took Jesus into my heart October 23, 1949. Amen. Praise the Lord.' He was just like a miniature grown-up.

Teddy walked across the open space to his seat. A twin nodded his head at me. He didn't smile. The nod was a command. I got up. I watched the patterns in the rug move under me as I walked to the center of the room. I glanced up. Three kids in front were messing around, slapping each other and giggling; another was staring out the window; two older boys at the back looked at me, then at each other. I turned toward the twins. The same one nodded sharply. His eyebrows came down. I looked at the carpet again. Ground-in dirt muddied its rust color.

'I gave – I-I gave my heart to Jesus.' I looked sideways at the twin. Eyebrows bumped up. 'Today,' I said. 'November 3, na-na-nineteen forty-nine.'

I walked sideways back to my place watching dirt clouds puff up from the rug. It was a lie. They knew, I knew.

> **I walked sideways back to my place watching dirt clouds puff up from the rug. It was a lie. They knew. I knew**

Mrs Hanson picked us up in the station wagon. We didn't talk on the way home.

On the Thursday after I gave my heart to Jesus – or said those words – Mrs Hanson didn't come in the station wagon. I never went back to Bible school and I never found out why. Maybe the twins kicked me out; maybe Teddy told his mother I lied and she told my parents. Maybe my parents asked what happened and I said, 'I had to take Jesus into my heart,' and my father got mad and stopped me going. I don't remember. I am not sure that I ever knew.

Nobody once mentioned the Bible school again. Teddy didn't, his mom didn't, my parents didn't, and neither did I. Nothing, silence, not a word – just like Jesus. So I knew I'd failed. Failed the test of character. Done something wrong. I didn't know what, I only knew I didn't go there anymore, to the Bible school. I didn't want to go there anymore, but that in itself meant I was a miserable quitter. I couldn't stick it out, I couldn't believe in Jesus and I wasn't as good as Teddy and the other kids.

I built a shell around that failure to protect myself from its spreading and then I got on with things: school, mowing the lawn, playing Monopoly with Teddy, reading books in bed. I grew up and took a job at the paper office; then down in Newark with the Republicans where I was molested for the second time in my life.

It's just conceivable that the elevator operator is still alive. Looking back I see a youngish man, perhaps 25, perhaps 30, shiny dark hair, narrow face, classical nose, soft brown eyes. He might have been a war veteran, World War Two or Korea. He had a job with a future, at the National Newark and Essex Bank Building where money pumped like ruby blood through the heart of commerce. He wore a uniform, worked inside, might one day have been promoted to captain.

Poor man! When I shouted whatever I shouted – 'Quit it, you fuck!' – he leapt away from me and switched on the light. He looked scared. He hadn't forced anything, hadn't wrestled with me, hadn't hit me. I think now he must have deluded himself in that curious way humans have in matters of affection. You impute to another your own feelings. You see in the other person's eyes the fire that burns in your own, as in a false mirror. He was attracted to me; he thought I was to him. And why not? I smiled and said, 'Hi,' when I got in his car.

I listened and talked with him, I was grateful when a grown-up was friendly. I had tousled hair and bright blue eyes and smooth cheeks. Who wouldn't be interested?

In just a few years the elevators' manual control panels would be replaced by self-service buttons and the operators in their uniforms would vanish from the cars. The sweet order imposed by the captain would deteriorate into the world of pushing and jostling, squeezing and muttering that most indoor workers in tall buildings now associate with vertical travel at peak hours. And what might have seemed a lifetime job would be gone. Still, I cost him that job before technology and the drive for profits took it away.

The sweet order imposed by the captain would deteriorate into the world of pushing and jostling, squeezing and muttering that most workers now associate with vertical travel

At that time the twins would have been grown-ups knocking at the old people's door. By now they will certainly have been dead for many years. At some point in my life – parked at night on a quiet street with my girlfriend, or in college when I read *Portrait of the Artist as a Young Man* – at some point I understood that the twins could have hurt me but they didn't get me. I hadn't failed, I'd won. I had passed the test of character. The obvious lie I was forced to tell said it all – I didn't believe. They were after my mind and they didn't get it. The child is a born and budding empiricist. He tests his world, he's true to his senses, he draws lessons from experience. He is also greatly in the sway of adults who manipulate love and fear like tongs to bring him to belief. That's where I had won, even if I had lied in victory.

Now I wish I'd let the elevator operator keep his job and instead told on the twins. But who would a kid tell, anyway? **H**

Double page spread, full colour £350

Single page, full colour £200

Half page, full colour £120

Single page, b&w — £150

Half page, b&w — £70

To take advantage of the above rates and advertise with Hinterland, or to discuss sponsorship or other collaborations, please contact Andrew Kenrick: hinterlandnonfiction@gmail.com

HINTERLAND

Hinterland publishes the bestselling authors you know and love, as well as the fresh new voices of tomorrow. Our readers are intelligent, creative and curious. If this is the company you'd like to keep, consider advertising your product or service with us.

IN CONVERSATION WITH
Bart van Es

Hinterland editors Freya Dean and Andrew Kenrick travelled to Oxford on a rainy day in May to interview author of The Cut Out Girl, *Bart van Es, in a conversation that considered W.H. Sebald, the role of memory in writing and the chastening parallels between mid-century Europe and the world today.*

Andrew: Had the idea of writing *The Cut Out Girl* been percolating for a while? Early on in the book you describe a conversation with your mother, where you say that you'd been aware of this family history for a long time and that your uncle's death galvanised you to really look into it.

Bart: Yes, but that was only a retrospective realisation I think. I had always been aware that my grandparents were part of the resistance and vaguely aware that there had been this Jewish girl, Lien, who had come to live with them after the war. I was even more vaguely aware that there had been this row – I remember my mother crying about it – but none of it had ever crystallised into a concrete set of facts.

I suppose if I really look back, I first thought I ought to record it in some way when I went to Cambridge (as an undergraduate) and started meeting a lot of people who talked about being Jewish. That was the first time I began to think about that history in a concrete way because in my world people didn't really describe themselves as Jewish – it just felt like this category from the Second World War. Sometimes I would say that my grandparents had done things in the war, but then I felt uncomfortable talking about it because I didn't know what their contribution actually was.

But I do think it was the death of my uncle in November 2014, combined with the rise of fake news and a new extremism and signs of a new anti-Semitism, Islamic State… all those things did make that history feel more relevant. Then once I'd had that conversation with my mother I became really determined to find out about it, but even then it wasn't really a plan – when I pressed that doorbell in Amsterdam and Lien asked me 'what's your motivation?' I didn't really know. I didn't have a plan.

Freya: So she asked you that at the outset?

BvE: Yes she did – and she said 'what kind of book?' And by that point I'd written her an email saying maybe a book but I'd thought it could also have been the basis for an academic article, some kind of family memoir…

AK: Was it always the plan to write something as a result of it?

BvE: Always a piece of writing but not necessarily a piece of creative non-fiction. It could have grown into a record, like something on the Shoah

Foundation archives. But then the thing that utterly overwhelmed me was that first day with Lien; she very quickly said that she had faith in it, that she wanted to do it. I'd come for half an hour and was still there ten hours later. I heard in incredibly vivid detail about that farewell meeting when she saw her relatives for the last time and it just haunted me. I thought, I've got to record this and knew then that it had to be in some way that would make it vivid, that it wouldn't be just the bare facts.

AK: Did you sense on that day that she'd been waiting for the opportunity to tell it?

BvE: Not at all, no. She was very emphatic that she didn't have a story when we first met. Nothing special happened to her, she said, which is kind of amazing; and yet, in another sense, you can see what she means because there are thousands of people with similar experiences and hundreds of thousands if you put it in the wider context. So she didn't have that sense at all and I think that actually made her easier to interview because she was very neutral. I caught her at a moment when she was totally at ease with the story, which is not how she had lived her life. She'd had a life defined by the trauma of survival but, as you read in the book, she had made that very decisive move to say: I'm going to be happy and for me it's in the past. So that put me in a really privileged position interviewing her. She was interested in recording it and was actually very joyous about it – at a certain point in the midst of our interviews she was on the phone to her daughter saying 'Bart's asked such interesting questions, I didn't think I could remember so much about it.' So it did spark a lot of things for her but not in a way that was ever traumatic.

The only time she said it really hit her was when she read the Dutch translation of the book. I had sent her the English version and she was able to puzzle out the sentences to say whether it was right, that the facts were correct, but when she read the Dutch version she said she had had to lie down for a few days because then it was an immersive experience. One that was her own but also not, because although the details were as true as they could be, she was also aware that there was someone else's imagination at play.

FD: It sounds like the thing that every writer aims to achieve when they treat their own life material – that distance, when you're looking at events almost dispassionately.

BvE: Absolutely. Lien would say that she doesn't focus on the past now – she has friends who look at their parents' photographs every day and she says she's decided not to do that because she doesn't want to be defined by the experience. She recognises that her parents wouldn't have wanted that, that her relatives wouldn't have wanted it.

AK: So in some respects if you'd met her sooner, this book wouldn't have been the outcome?

BvE: It really wouldn't have. The woman who had the row with my grandmother or who grew up after the war with the van Eses would have been extremely difficult to talk to. In the book I mention those two parallel bits of film. One where Lien is being interviewed for Spielberg's project, which is in the mid-nineties –

FD: Where she's watching herself on the television screen?

BvE: Yes. She looks physically older in that film than she does now. Lien had said that she was nervous of looking at it again, there was this real sense of discomfort. She'd told me that it was because she hadn't liked the questions they were asking, but when we looked at the tape together, she said actually it wasn't their questions so much as it was her.

AK: To what extent did it feel like a collaborative effort? In the book it seems as if you worked very closely together.

BvE: There are different ways of answering that. It felt intensely collaborative as I was doing the interviews. I would come back with photographs and new facts and they would then form the basis of further interviews; so that initial month was very collaborative. I would also phone her up as I was writing – we would have Skype conversations – and I would say 'can you say anything more about this–?'

On the other hand Lien always said 'it's your book' and she trusted me with it. So she intervened very, very little once we'd finished the interviews. I would always show her the chapters and there were maybe only three paragraphs, which detailed her stay with the Heromas in Dordrecht, that she wanted me to change.

FD: I want to ask about the photographs in the book. They've been compared to the way that WG Sebald uses images, but it struck me that it's actually quite a different thing that you're doing. In Sebald's books the photographs have a destabilising effect on the narrative, they can be very disorientating; whereas I felt that the way you use photographs – although they are scattered throughout the text in a similar way – they have a very different effect of reaffirming the writing and forcing the reader to remember that this happened, that it isn't a story. I wondered if that was your intention?

BvE: That's really interesting because I *was* influenced by Sebald but yes, his books are fundamentally defined by this really dreamy, almost nauseous consciousness. *Austerlitz*, *Rings of Saturn* and *The Emigrants* are all in that same mode. If I was going to be critical of Sebald I think he doesn't really give much room for the actual identity of his protagonists – they are all part of that apparently directionless swinging into nineteenth century history.

I wanted all the photographs to be of the things that Lien showed me, I didn't include any photographs I took or add any documents I'd found. So they are there to show the artefacts that Lien had and I suppose the scaffolding around which I built the story – so you're right, they are much more concrete objects than the de-contextualised ephemera that Sebald is interested in.

On the other hand I did want to have that Sebaldian thing of not labelling photographs, because I really didn't want the book to feel like a biography with footnotes; Lien's experience of the war wasn't like that. Some people have asked why isn't there a family tree, why isn't there a chronology, why isn't there a map? I felt quite strongly that I didn't want those in the book, because that's not how Lien lived it. There's no sense of the war lasting from 1939-45 for her as a child; if I were to give the reader a tidy list of dates that becomes very distorting.

AK: Was there ever the temptation to limit the book to that period of her life? Was there any pressure to write it in a more conventional way?

BvE: Well, in terms of her life, I could have imagined writing a piece about her war experiences when I first met her, but then after I spent a month with her in January 2015 that changed. It was for me just this utterly overwhelming experience and it was also my personal experience of travelling across the Netherlands and these things that emerged from the apparently un-contoured Dutch landscape. That here is a family tragedy about a girl who went off to Israel, or there is a Muslim family now living opposite where a Jewish girl was in hiding. At the end of that month I was very clear that I wanted to capture what I had just experienced. Which was partly an intense identification with someone else's story – that amazing privilege of having someone's life story from the age of 2 to 82 – but also my journey.

Structurally it changed, so the way that it is now with really those three voices cutting into each other, occluded the first-person narration. It became Lien's life, my biographical narrative and then this omniscient historical voice.

FD: In a sense your voice and Lien's hold each other to account – I can't imagine it without that dynamic.

BvE: No, but that did take quite a while to work out. At the beginning there were bigger blocks. I wrote the early chapters of Lien's life first, immediately after doing the interviews and then I had quite a long period of thinking about the structure.

A friend put me in touch with a literary agent, David Miller and he was like a creative writing tutor, really. He told me to read. He gave me Fred Uhlman's *Reunion*, which I'd read before but now read again, and a certain amount of Dutch fiction. He said 'think about what the emotional heart of this story is for you.' So I'd planned it to have bigger chronological blocks so that you'd get Lien's story at the beginning and then a kind of flashback to how I got to meet her. And it wasn't that David told me to intercut them the way they are now, but he gave me the space to think about that.

There was quite a long period – May 2015 to January 2016 – when I wasn't writing anything.

AK: You were just reading?

BvE: Reading and planning... we wrote up the proposal for the book. A long document of about 18 pages which in a lot of ways acted as a complete structural plan. Once I had that, I then wrote pretty much solidly on the book for the next 18 months.

FD: You've just touched on that thread of contemporary Netherlands – the book is really a portrait of that as well. I'm thinking of that moment when you're driving and all the container lorries are going past and there's this real sense of haunting, but it's something we rarely talk about. That was startling to me, that that's exactly how it is – we travel up and down these same routes and yet pretend that nothing happened.

BvE: It's particularly intense there in Ijsselmonde because it had been this complete backwater and now it's the most industrial space that you can imagine; yet there is still this little historical cluster that is unchanged. That, combined with the fact that as I was driving the Charlie Hebdo attacks were reported on the radio – which happened exactly as I described in the book – that was a very Sebaldian feeling for me. There it was quite dizzying: the palimpsest of past and present that's at the heart of so much of Sebald's work. At that moment I was thinking: I don't have a real sense of where I am. I was so intensely in Lien's experience at the same time that I was being overwhelmed by modernity and yet a kind of atavistic return to those things.

AK: You mentioned that moment in 2014 when it crystallised for you that you needed to write this book, and you talk about the growing threats, or the perceived threats, at that time. Those threats only seem to have grown stronger in the time since you've written it.

BvE: It's true. I couldn't have imagined we'd have a Labour party member chanting 'death to Israel,' who the leader refuses to condemn, and the President of America talking about the 'many good people on both sides.' That very frightening idea of truth being negotiable, a kind of stunning return to a Goebbels world where somebody is just saying 'no, this didn't happen.'

AK: The book is a very timely reminder of how those battles were won – or not won – in the first place.

FD: And particularly in the UK there's a singular, dominant narrative around the Second World War with the result that those stories acquire the quality of myth and very few people will challenge that narrative, or be critical of it.

BvE: Yes and the myths are even stronger in the Netherlands than in the UK. There's a way in which what happened in 1943 ended up defining the Dutch experience of the war. Once Dutch men were being sent to forced-labour camps in Germany and once it was becoming clear the Allies were going to win the war, then suddenly everyone thought of it as an occupation.

But in 1942 people didn't think of it as 'The War'. That made me far more admiring of my grandparents than I had been before. They didn't think they would be looking after these children until the end of the war in 1945; they assumed that the Nazis would always be there and that this was a new Europe – it was forever. You see then this sense of mythic power, the full epic scale of an individual versus an enormous flood. That courage makes me quite emotional to think about, that act of faith – we're still going to do what's right – when everything was pushing people to accept the situation.

I don't like to think of literature as something that gives lessons, but in a way it does. There are very big forces at work now – climate change, for example – that actually do depend on individuals recognising that this is an enormous, terrifying thing that's coming towards us. And OK that's not the same because you have to be very careful what you compare to the Holocaust, but on the other hand it still takes people to say 'this looks impossible, but this is a defining moment and we cannot carry on as we are.'

FD: Those moments of collective choice.

BvE: Yes.

FD: What has the reaction been within the Netherlands to what is really your revision of this period of Dutch history?

BvE: The book is now more prominent in the UK than the Netherlands, but initially its reception was a Dutch one. When it came out Lien and I appeared on Dutch national television and the letter [that Lien's mother wrote to the couple who would receive Lien] was read out on the programme *Pauw*. That had a huge impact on the people who watched it, to see that in living memory such a letter could be written.

Also Lien was very determined to give the book political purchase. She'd made this direct, brave link with two Armenian children, Lili and Howick. This was already a cause celebrè: two children aged twelve and thirteen, who had arrived in the Netherlands as refugees and entirely grown up there – they had no Armenian language – but who were now going to be sent back to an Armenian orphanage, because the country had been declared safe. The Dutch foreign minister said that people are genetically incapable of multiculturalism – that was actually something that he said. So Lien speaking out against that and saying if you want to know what's going to happen to those children, look at my story, that had a big impact towards the reversal of that decision.

The book is not that prominent now but it was referenced recently in a piece about the attack on Mari Andriessen's statue of the Dock Worker in Amsterdam. The statue commemorates the February '41 national strike organised by the unions against the deportation of Jews. This was one real point of light during the Dutch occupation – the Netherlands was the one country that organised a national strike – but then it was cracked down on incredibly viciously, with people on the picket lines just being shot. Which does partly help to explain how difficult the choice of resistance was. That same statue was recently spattered with paint by some anti-Semitic football supporters, and an editorial in the NRC (a Dutch newspaper) said we need to read *The Cut Out Girl* to remember that this country doesn't quite have this smug narrative.

AK: Were the Dutch and English editions released in parallel?

BvE: Yes, within a week of each other. I worked on the Dutch text for quite a lot of the time that I was copy editing the English one.

F: So did you write both?

BvE: No, but I was pretty involved in it. When the text was first translated into Dutch it was in a way that I wasn't happy with at all. I didn't feel that they'd captured what I was trying to do with the child's voice; so then I spent three months working on the Dutch text, sent it back and asked that it go to a second translator because I'm not capable of writing really literary Dutch prose.

AK: What has the reaction been within Lien's family and your own?

BvE: I've been so lucky with that. My parents were very worried about it and there were things my dad didn't want me to put in the book that I did put in, which was very difficult emotionally. Throughout the time of writing my parents were extremely unhappy with the fact I was doing this, though they didn't try and stop me.

FD: Did you send them excerpts to read? That's a really tough decision when you write about other people –

BvE: Particularly if you send them stuff and say that you're really not prepared to change it. Although I did discuss things with them and as a result there were some very minor changes that I made… so there is always that element of compromise.

FD: Although your family and Lien's family are enmeshed in the story, the book also rises far above that – it's certainly not a family biography in any sense.

BvE: No – the first line 'without families you don't get stories' is universally true, and it's something you can only begin to understand by the time you get to the end of the book. It's an incredible moment of wisdom for Lien that actually things almost don't happen to you if you don't have someone to share them with.

It's why that early part of the war is very vivid to her – she had people to share stories with, to laugh with, to cry over things, that's why the van Eses' world is so vivid to her. But if you're a child on your own in Ijsselmonde or Bennekom and there's nobody you laugh with, huge sections just fall away. That's something very interesting about what family gives you. Lien used to say to people that she was born after the war. The mid-life trauma that she had was partly the way the past forced itself back on her. When she became a mother she could no longer block out the memory of her own mother.

AK: There was a part I was particularly struck by – on the walk from Ede when they pass that crater in the road. That whole scene is so vividly described and then you tell the reader 'Lien doesn't have any memory of this.' How did you manage that – was it through interviewing other people? Was it through your imagination – what was your process in writing those scenes?

BvE: That is a really important bit because that journey from Bennekom to Ede is actually the only bit of the book where you can absolutely say that Lien has no memory at all. She very much remembers the parachutes coming down and has vivid memories of hiding in the cellar and hearing bullets, but then there's just this period of complete blank.
This came to me as a complete revelation when I went to the de Bond's house in Bennekom and they said 'Lien spent two weeks here.' Up until that

point Lien and I had assumed we could build on her memory, but then there was this really very memorable event with another whole family that she has no memory of – this was a very major shock to me and I thought OK, I've got to work differently.

I interviewed the de Bonds and they added this whole extra history. I talked to Corrie, who remembered the journey, as did lots of other people who have written about it in their own journals. There's a whole world of family histories in the Netherlands – small, local journals often published by a town or village – and something like the crater or the horse with the flies, those are lifted from those accounts. So it was possible for me to reconstruct the journey very vividly on the basis of other people's memories and I thought it would be quite a salutary moment in the book to give you that very clear description at that point.

AK: Because you don't preface it – that this is what you're doing – it's very unsettling. How early on was it in the process that you discovered Lien had these memory absences?

BvE: That happened in late January when I went to Bennekom. On one level I'd sort of thought I knew what I was doing. Up until then it had been relatively predictable: I would go to the flat in the Hague, I would go to my grandparents' former house in Dordrecht, and it made sense. I was getting the geography right, I was talking to people. But then suddenly… it was a real trap-door-opening-under-you moment.

There were 150 Jews hidden in this tiny village. My grandparents lived in this village, I've been to this village all my life, my aunt and uncle live up the road – none of them knew about this. And I just thought: how could this be? In Britain there would at least be a local war memorial, there would be a historical society that talked about it, but here… absolutely nothing. So then you realise that the amnesia is also a national amnesia. There's the personal amnesia of Lien, but also you realise this is a country that's traumatised, that has had to create a false memory of universal resistance. However, that memory itself is very opaque. Stories of resistance were not recorded after the war, because your neighbours mostly did nothing and your stories were not going to be welcome. Many of them collaborated, many turned a blind eye and when the war was over it was 'hooray so now we're going to rebuild, it's going to be different.'

AK: What was the moment that galvanised your grandmother to take in Lien?

BvE: I think it was because my grandparents were part of something bigger than themselves, which I think is another major take away from this story. They had always been part of a campaigning, activist network. My grandfather was a trade union leader and particularly in '42 it was very largely the trade unions who acted. The Heromas were part of that same political party, the SDAP [Social Democratic Workers Party] – which was really a forerunner for the Dutch Labour party - and they had a political awareness of Nazi Germany that stretched much further back. Already throughout the 1930s they were describing themselves as 'antifascist.'

Though I hardly ever discussed it with my grandmother, I do remember her saying 'we weren't brave, what were you going to do if they put a child on your doorstep?' But they wouldn't have put a child at the door of my mother's parents. I don't think they were less moral people than my father's parents, but they were not political, they didn't have that wider horizon.

Woven through the book is that sense of absolute conviction in socialism, which shaped so much of the positive resistance to Nazism, but which then had its moments of disillusionment after the boom years of the 1960s.

FD: I found that really moving; the depression your grandmother sunk into, that feeling of loss when you believe so fiercely in something and see it being unpicked.

BvE: And after the war they really thought that this was a utopia that they were going to build. It's going to be clean, efficient, with libraries, swimming pools. You can see that vision... these lovely new houses, these flats, it's going to be perfect. Then it was like a switch that was flicked off in the 1970s. America went off the gold standard and suddenly Japan is competition, and all of these things that looked new five years earlier now look shabby. Decades sometimes really do become these hard borders.

The Cut Out Girl *is out now in paperback from Penguin.* **H**

Like what you've read?

Look out for the third issue of Hinterland, on sale November 2019. Better still, sign up for a subscription and get our next batch of stand-out writing delivered direct to your door, desktop or tablet.

Annual print & digital subscription £34
Four issues, saving £6 off list price

Annual digital subscription £20
Four issues, saving £4 off list price

Subscribers also enjoy the benefits of being able to submit their writing to Hinterland free of charge.

Visit our website to subscribe:

www.hinterlandnonfiction.com/subscribe